THE FEDERALIST

PAPERS

A MODERN LANGUAGE

TRANSLATION IN PARALLEL

TEXT

Federalist Papers Numbers 1, 10, 39, 51, 53,

70, 78

TRANSLATED BY GENEVIEVE GILBERT-ROLFE

For my son, Cedric, to whom the torch has been passed, and my granddaughter, Leiah, in whose eyes I see the future

James Madison served as the 4th president of the U.S. from 1809 to 1817 and as 5th Secretary of State under Thomas Jefferson. He is considered the "Father of the Constitution" as well as the Bill of Rights because of his role in writing and promoting them. He co-wrote The Federalist Papers. This is the short list of his accomplishments.

TRANSLATOR'S NOTE

After several years of shepherding students through readings of the Federalist Papers, and losing many of them along the way, I decided that the dated language of the Papers was getting in the way. I began these translations with *Federalist #39*, one of the most important of the essays and also one of the most difficult for the modern reader to understand.

Aided with a modern language version, my students finally succeeded in understanding Madison's arguments. Some read only the modern language version; some read the original referring to the modern language column only when it was necessary; and some intrepid scholars insisted on reading only the original. Having the choice allowed them to learn in a way most suitable to themselves. The usefulness of making these translations was apparent to me from the success of my students.

The Papers selected for translation include those most frequently assigned in courses on U.S. Government or U.S. History. They cover the most essential principles and institutions of our government.

The "Guided Reading Questions" have been included to help the student (and the general reader as well) focus on important points in each section of the *Paper*. Reading a paragraph or two and then stopping to answer a question, slows down the reader but also produces a more thoughtful consideration of the material. Paragraphs are numbered to facilitate comparisons between the original and the modern versions. In addition, a few paragraph breaks have been added to the original and the modern versions in order to make the text more readable. Each original *Federalist Paper* ends with the pen-name of the authors, PUBLIUS. Each modern version of that paper ends with my pen-name, Friend of PUBLIUS.

I have tried to be faithful to the original words as well as to the general meaning and purpose of each essay. However, I was constantly reminded, by the difficult decisions that had to be made, that every translation is also an interpretation.

TABLE OF CONTENTS

Federalist #1

This essay explains why a new constitution is needed, and why the changes should not be feared.

Federalist #10

This *Paper* focuses primarily on the problem of special interest groups.

Federalist #39

This is an in-depth discussion of the nature of federalism as a system of shared sovereignty.

Federalist #51

This *Paper* discusses separation of powers and checks and balances.

Federalist #53

This essay is an argument for longer terms of office and a more powerful national government.

Federalist #70

This essay concerns the structure and power of the presidency.

Federalist #78

This essay is an argument in favor of a strong and independent judiciary.

Alexander Hamilton served as senior aide to George Washington in the
Revolution, wrote 51 of the 85 Federalist Papers. Later, he became the first
and is the youngest ever Secretary of the Treasury. This is the short list of
his accomplishments.

Forward

The Federalist Papers: A Translation

With the exception of the Constitution itself, there are no more significant documents in America's political history than The Federalist Papers, which provide the most authoritative interpretation and commentary on the Constitution, the leading law of the land that is available to us. The Constitution is brief. It establishes the broad principles of governance in the United States but it does not give reasons for its various provisions nor explain what they mean and why they are important. The Federalist Papers, written by Alexander Hamilton, James Madison, and John Jay, explicate the meaning of the Constitution.

Despite our deep political polarization, politicians, judges, and citizens on every side of the political spectrum claim a fidelity to constitutional principles. As such it makes good sense to understand what the framers said and what they meant when they wrote those majestic words more than 200 years ago. Genevieve Gilbert-Rolfe's modern language translation of The Federalist Papers is a wonderful place to start.

The first plan of national government in the United States was not the Constitution, however, but was instead the Articles of Confederation. Ratified in 1781, the Articles guided the new American nation after its war of independence with Great Britain. The Articles of Confederation vested political power in the hands of state government because many Americas believed that a too powerful national government would threaten their liberty. Under the Articles, the national government could neither tax nor regulate interstate or foreign commerce, and the Articles could only be amended with the unanimous agreement of the Congress and the assent of all the state legislatures, a virtually impossible task.

Political and social problems mounted in America and it became clear to many that the national government under the Articles of Confederation had neither the economic nor the military power to function effectively. On February 2, 1787 the Continental Congress resolved that: "on the second Monday in May a Convention of delegates who shall have been appointed by the several States be held in Philadelphia for the sole and express purpose of revising the Articles of Confederation."

Convinced that a simple revision of The Articles was insufficient for the problems at hand, the delegates drafted a new Constitution setting up a stronger national government for the states. Before it could take effect, however, a minimum of nine state conventions had to ratify the Constitution and the process of selling it to the people began. The newspapers of the day became the battleground for a remarkable series of articles supporting and opposing ratification of the Constitution.

The proponents of ratification, calling themselves Federalists, published eighty-five articles in New York newspapers beginning in October of 1787. The purpose of these articles was to convince the voting public that the

Constitution could strengthen the power of the national government without threatening the liberties of the colonists or the political sovereignty of the states.

The Federalist Papers make clear that the Constitution accomplishes this delicate balancing act through a system of federalism, checks and balances, separation of powers, political pluralism, and representative government. The genius of the new political system is that although the national government is given power sufficient to insure social and political order, the structure of the government makes "an unjust combination of a majority of the whole, very improbable (*Federalist #51*)." According to the authors, Madison, Hamilton, and Jay, the Constitution demands compromise among the various branches of government. Because of the fragmentation of political power, private interests would have to be surrendered in order that coalitions could be built. This process, in their view, would preserve the basic rights of American citizens while at the same time establishing a national government strong enough to respond to the social and political challenges of the day.

In her modern language translation of The Federalist Papers, Genevieve Gilbert-Rolfe has made a significant contribution to the study of the Constitution for high school and college students and the general reader alike. Her translation makes these core American documents accessible to readers in a way that they have never been before. The quality of the paraphrasing is consistently very high; she retains the essential arguments of The Federalist

Papers in this book but does so in a way that readers will find much easier to understand.

Contemporary events have contributed to political polarization, dysfunction, and widespread distrust of the government. There is even a growing concern about the future of American democracy and our republican form of government. Reading The Federalist Papers is no panacea for our current challenges, but it can provide a healthy reminder that our country has faced challenges before and that the structure and principles upon which a government is based greatly affect the political outcomes that we can expect from it. Genevieve Gilbert-Rolfe has done us all a great service by making the arguments and insights about our Constitution from the past accessible to us in the present.

J. Christopher Soper
Distinguished Professor of Political Science
Pepperdine University

Author's INTRODUCTION to the Volume

· ·

The Federalist Papers are a collection of eighty-five essays written by James Madison, Alexander Hamilton and John Jay. They were published between October 27, 1787 and August 16, 1788 in various newspapers in New York City. The announced purpose of the papers was to convince the people of New York State to support the Constitution that had been drafted in Philadelphia in 1787. This new plan of union would completely replace the Articles of Confederation, which had been in official use since 1781.

The Articles had created a confederacy, a loose association of sovereign states. The central government had only one branch, which was the Continental Congress, and also lacked sufficient power to run the country effectively. Laws required agreement by at least nine of the thirteen States, which rarely occurred. There was no executive to see that the laws were faithfully executed. There was no national court system to resolve peacefully the legal claims among the States and their respective citizens. To fix the shortcomings of The Articles, all thirteen States had to agree to any changes. The new nation had been unable to maintain an adequate defense against foreign invasion or interference, nor had it been able to establish a stable economy following the end of the Revolutionary War.

The new Constitution proposed at the Philadelphia Convention of 1787 created a strong central government, which would, for the first time, truly unify the thirteen separate States into a single nation. The new plan of government proposed something unique in the history of political unions, a united country within which semi-autonomous states would be guaranteed authority over their own territories. That combination of what today we would call unitary and confederal governments became known as "federalism," and it has served as a model for many nations seeking to combine the benefits of local preference with the strength of centralized power.

The new central government, whose capital would be distant from the people and whose institutions (except for the House of Representatives) would be placed beyond their direct control, inspired fear and distrust in many hearts. The framers of the Constitution themselves sought to contain and control the new government's powers by dividing it among three branches, providing each branch with the motive and ability to block excesses by the other two. The authors of The Federalist Papers asserted that the new Constitution would create a limited government with strength and accountability.

Throughout The Federalist Papers, Hamilton and Madison (due to illness, John Jay's contribution was limited) demonstrate the extent to which the new Constitution sought to find the middle ground between individual freedom and social order, between self-interest and the public good, between the power of the individual States and the powers of the new nation-state, between majority rule and minority rights, between an oppressively strong government and a government too weak to be effective.

In other words they faced squarely, and for the most part candidly, the problems that had in the past, and would in the future, face all representative democracies. The lessons they teach us have many applications. Their philosophical insights into the nature of man in a political setting are as useful today as they were in 1787. In short, The Federalist Papers are as valuable for their honesty and wisdom as they are for their analysis and arguments in favor of the single and fundamental document of our nation, the United States Constitution.

THE FORMAL DELIVERY OF THE STATUE.

The statue is of Libertas, a Roman goddess of liberty. She was given to the people of the U.S. in 1886 by the people of France to commemorate the centennial of the Revolution. In her right hand she holds a torch as a beacon to the world and in her left hand, a tablet dated July 4, 1776. A broken shackle and chain lie at her feet celebrating the end of slavery in the U.S in 1865. She has become a global symbol of the promise of freedom.

Author's Introduction to
THE FEDERALIST #1
General Introduction for the
Independent Journal
October 27, 1787

· ·

·

The *Federalist #1* is an introduction to the whole series of eighty-five essays written by Alexander Hamilton, James Madison and John Jay, which we now call The Federalist Papers. These essays were originally published in several New York City newspapers. Alexander Hamilton wrote this essay, *Federalist #1,* and addressed it to the people of New York State in order to persuade New Yorkers to support the new Constitution. New York had a large population and it was strategically located between the two most important States, Massachusetts and Virginia.

If New York did not vote to join the United States, the new country would be split in half. The opposition to the Constitution in New York, led by Governor George Clinton was strong and well organized. The writers of The Federalist Papers had to argue forcefully and persuasively. After their original appearance in newspapers, the eighty-five essays were printed as a collection and were studied and discussed then, as they are now, in schools, universities, courts and foreign countries, as the best available analysis of federalist, representative democracies such as ours.

Terms to know before you read the essay: (see Glossary)

- Tyrant
- Confederacy
- Demagogue
- Republican government
- Articles of Confederation
- Federal

GUIDED READING QUESTIONS for
Students to answer as you read

1. What question do the people of the U.S. seem destined to answer for all mankind?

2. Why is it unlikely that the people of the U.S. will make their decision about ratifying the new Constitution based only on what is best for the country?

3. What will motivate those who oppose the new Constitution?

4. Why should we be tolerant toward those who have opposing views on this subject (or any subject for that matter)?

5. Why should we distrust those who advocate liberty more than those who propose a strong and efficient government?

6. What does Hamilton reveal about his own point of view?

7. Reading over the list of topics that will be discussed in the other Federalist Papers, what do you think are the positive characteristics of the Constitution?

8. Why is it useful to begin the Federalist Papers with a discussion of the benefits of unifying the states if, as Hamilton says, most people already agreed with that idea?

To the People of the State of New York:

[1]AFTER an unequivocal experience of the inefficiency of the subsisting federal government, you are called upon to deliberate on a new Constitution for the United States of America. The subject speaks its own importance; comprehending in its consequences nothing less than the existence of the UNION, the safety and welfare of the parts of which it is composed, the fate of an empire in many respects the most interesting in the world. It has been frequently remarked that it seems to have been reserved to the people of this country, by their conduct and example, to decide the important question, whether societies of men are really capable or not of establishing good government from reflection and choice, or whether they are forever destined to depend for their political constitutions on accident and force. If there be any truth in the remark, the crisis at which we are

MODERN version of Federalist #1

To the People of the State of New York:

[1]HAVING experienced the undeniable inefficiency of the current national government, you are now called upon to consider carefully a new constitution for the United States. This is obviously an important question because the very existence of the nation depends on it. The answer will determine the safety and welfare of the parts that make up the whole of the Union, and the fate of an nation that in many respects is the most interesting in the world. It is often said that the people of this country are fated to answer, by their actions and example, the question of whether societies are capable of establishing good government based on their own ideas and their own free choices. Or whether, on the other hand, mankind must forever depend on chance or force to establish a government for it? If America is truly destined to answer this question, then the present crisis should

arrived may with propriety be regarded as the era in which that decision is to be made; and a wrong election of the part we shall act may, in this view, deserve to be considered as the general misfortune of mankind.

(2)This idea will add the inducements of philanthropy to those of patriotism, to heighten the solicitude which all considerate and good men must feel for the event. Happy will it be if our choice should be directed by a judicious estimate of our true interests, unperplexed and unbiased by considerations not connected with the public good. But this is a thing more ardently to be wished than seriously to be expected. The plan offered to our deliberations affects too many particular interests, innovates upon too many local institutions, not to involve in its discussion a variety of objects foreign to its merits, and of views, passions and prejudices little favorable to the discovery of truth.

be considered the right time to do so. If we decide wrongly, it will truly be considered a misfortune for all mankind.

(2)The idea that our decision will affect everyone increases the concern of thoughtful and good men by adding the love of humanity to the love of country. How good it would be if we made our choice according to a wise estimate of the true interests of our country without being confused or biased by anything that is not connected with the public good. Alas, that is something to be strongly hoped for rather than to be seriously expected. The proposed Constitution effects so many special interests and makes changes to so many established laws and practices at the local level that rather than being judged on its own merits, people are bound to bring up many irrelevant points, strong emotions and prejudices which do not lead to a discovery of the truth.

ORIGINAL of FEDERALIST # 1

[3]Among the most formidable of the obstacles which the new Constitution will have to encounter may readily be distinguished the obvious interest of a certain class of men in every State to resist all changes which may hazard a diminution of the power, emolument, and consequence of the offices they hold under the State establishments; and the perverted ambition of another class of men, who will either hope to aggrandize themselves by the confusions of their country, or will flatter themselves with fairer prospects of elevation from the subdivision of the empire into several partial confederacies than from its union under one government.

[4]It is not, however, my design to dwell upon observations of this nature. I am well aware that it would be disingenuous to resolve indiscriminately the opposition of any set of men (merely because their situations might subject them to suspicion) into interested

MODERN version of FEDERALIST # 1

[3]Among the greatest obstacles faced by the new Constitution will be the obvious resistance of a certain group of men who will try to stop anything that would diminish the power, the salaries or the importance of the offices they presently hold at the State level. There will also be resistance from corrupt, ambitious men who hope to profit from conflict and confusion, as well as from those who believe that they will be more successful in a country subdivided into parts than in a country united under one government.

[4]It is not my intention, however, to spend much time on that subject. I am well aware that it would be unfair to dismiss the objections of whole groups of men because they might potentially be motivated by selfishness or greed. We must honestly admit

ORIGINAL of FEDERALIST # 1

or ambitious views. Candor will oblige us to admit that even such men may be actuated by upright intentions; and it cannot be doubted that much of the opposition which has made its appearance, or may hereafter make its appearance, will spring from sources, blameless at least, if not respectable--the honest errors of minds led astray by preconceived jealousies and fears. So numerous indeed and so powerful are the causes which serve to give a false bias to the judgment, that we, upon many occasions, see wise and good men on the wrong as well as on the right side of questions of the first magnitude to society. This circumstance, if duly attended to, would furnish a lesson of moderation to those who are ever so much persuaded of their being in the right in any controversy.

MODERN version of FEDERALIST # 1

that such men might instead be motivated by honorable intentions. Also much of the opposition to the new Constitution will come from those who are blameless if not admirable. These are honest minds led astray by preconceived jealousies and fears. Indeed, there are so many and such powerful causes of biased judgment that we often see wise and good men on the wrong as well as on the right side of the most important political issues confronting society. If those who believe themselves to be on the right side in every argument would consider how often biased judgment leads good men astray, they would learn to be more reasonable.

ORIGINAL of FEDERALIST # 1

[5]*And a further reason for caution, in this respect, might be drawn from the reflection that we are not always sure that those who advocate the truth are influenced by purer principles than their antagonists. Ambition, avarice, personal animosity, party opposition, and many other motives not more laudable than these, are apt to operate as well upon those who support as those who oppose the right side of a question. Were there not even these inducements to moderation, nothing could be more ill-judged than that intolerant spirit which has, at all times, characterized political parties. For in politics, as in religion, it is equally absurd to aim at making proselytes by fire and sword. Heresies in either can rarely be cured by persecution.*

[6]*And yet, however just these sentiments will be allowed to be, we have already sufficient indications that it will happen in this as in all former cases of*

MODERN version of FEDERALIST # 1

[5]Furthermore, we should remember that those who are on the right side of the argument do not necessarily have purer motives than those who are on the wrong side. Those who support the right side are just as likely to be motivated by ambition, greed, personal hatreds, petty politics and many other equally unworthy impulses as those on the wrong side are. If this is not enough to encourage us to be more moderate and reasonable, then we should realize that nothing could be more unwise than to adopt the intolerant spirit that has always characterized party politics. For in politics, just as in religion, it is foolish to try to make converts through the use of fire and sword. Incorrect religious and political beliefs can rarely be cured by attacking those who hold those beliefs.

[6]And yet, even though we agree that it is wise to be reasonable and moderate, we already see that what has happened in all previous discussions of

great national discussion. A torrent of angry and malignant passions will be let loose. To judge from the conduct of the opposite parties, we shall be led to conclude that they will mutually hope to evince the justness of their opinions, and to increase the number of their converts by the loudness of their declamations and the bitterness of their invectives. An enlightened zeal for the energy and efficiency of government will be stigmatized as the offspring of a temper fond of despotic power and hostile to the principles of liberty. An over-scrupulous jealousy of danger to the rights of the people, which is more commonly the fault of the head than of the heart, will be represented as mere pretense and artifice, the stale bait for popularity at the expense of the public good.

(7)It will be forgotten, on the one hand, that jealousy is the usual concomitant of love, and that the noble enthusiasm of liberty is apt to be infected

MODERN version of FEDERALIST # 1

important national issues will also happen in this one. A torrent of anger and ill-will will be let loose. Judging from the conduct of our opponents, it is obvious that they all hope to show their fairness and to convert people to their position by the loudness of their voices and the bitterness of their verbal attacks. A sensible enthusiasm for an effective and efficient government will be misrepresented as a love of absolute power and a hatred of the principles of liberty. An overly protective defense of individual rights, which is more often a fault of the head than of the heart, will be misjudged as a hypocritical attempt to gain popularity at the expense of the well-being of the nation.

[7]On the one hand, it will be forgotten that over-protectiveness often goes with intense love, and that the love of freedom is too often infected with a narrow-minded and ungenerous lack of trust.

ORIGINAL of FEDERALIST # 1

with a spirit of narrow and illiberal distrust. On the other hand, it will be equally forgotten that the vigor of government is essential to the security of liberty; that, in the contemplation of a sound and well-informed judgment, their interest can never be separated; and that a dangerous ambition more often lurks behind the specious mask of zeal for the rights of the people than under the forbidden appearance of zeal for the firmness and efficiency of government. History will teach us that the former has been found a much more certain road to the introduction of despotism than the latter, and that of those men who have overturned the liberties of republics, the greatest number have begun their career by paying an obsequious court to the people; commencing demagogues, and ending tyrants.

(8In the course of the preceding observations, I have had an eye, my fellow-citizens, to putting you upon your guard against all attempts, from whatever quarter, to

MODERN version of FEDERALIST # 1

On the other hand, it will also be forgotten that a strong government is essential for the protection of freedom. In fact, if we judge with a rational and well-informed mind, we will see that a strong government and the safety of our freedom are inseparable. Dangerous ambition hides behind the misleading mask of a love of individual rights more often than it does behind the stern and unfriendly face of a love for strength and efficiency in government. History teaches us that dictatorships have more often been introduced by those claiming to protect liberty than by those claiming to strengthen government Of those men who have overturned the liberties of republics, most have begun their careers with a grand display of respect for the rights of the people, beginning as demagogues and ending as tyrants.

[8]In the course of this essay, my fellow citizens, I have attempted to alert you to be on guard against

ORIGINAL of FEDERALIST # 1

influence your decision in a matter of the utmost moment to your welfare, by any impressions other than those which may result from the evidence of truth.   You will, no doubt, at the same time, have collected from the general scope of them, that they proceed from a source not unfriendly to the new Constitution.   Yes, my countrymen, I own to you that, after having given it an attentive consideration, I am clearly of opinion it is your interest to adopt it.   I am convinced that this is the safest course for your liberty, your dignity, and your happiness.

(9)I affect not reserves which I do not feel.   I will not amuse you with an appearance of deliberation when I have decided.   I frankly acknowledge to you my convictions, and I will freely lay before you the reasons on which they are founded.   The consciousness of good intentions disdains ambiguity.   I shall not, however, multiply professions on this head.   My motives must remain in the depository of my own breast.

MODERN version of FEDERALIST # 1

all attempts, from whatever source, to influence your opinion with anything other than the truth on a matter of so much importance to your welfare. You will undoubtedly have noticed that my observations in this essay come from a point of view that is friendly to the new Constitution. Yes, my countrymen, I confess to you that after having given it careful consideration, I am clearly of the opinion that it is in your best interest to adopt the new Constitution. I am convinced that this is the safest thing to do for your liberty, your dignity, and your happiness.

[9]I have not pretended to have doubts that I do not really feel. I will not amuse you with hypothetical arguments, when I have, in fact, already decided. I frankly admit my convictions, and I will freely lay before you the reasons on which they are founded. Because of my strong belief in the task I have undertaken, I want to avoid being

ORIGINAL of FEDERALIST # 1

My arguments will be open to all, and may be judged of by all. They shall at least be offered in a spirit which will not disgrace the cause of truth.

[10]*I propose, in a series of papers, (that is, The Federalist Papers) to discuss the following interesting particulars:* THE UTILITY OF THE UNION TO YOUR POLITICAL PROSPERITY; THE INSUFFICIENCY OF THE PRESENT CONFEDERATION TO PRESERVE THAT UNION; THE NECESSITY OF A GOVERNMENT AT LEAST EQUALLY ENERGETIC WITH THE ONE PROPOSED. TO THE ATTAINMENT OF THIS OBJECT THE CONFORMITY OF THE PROPOSED CONSTITUTION TO THE TRUE PRINCIPLES OF REPUBLICAN GOVERNMENT ITS ANALOGY TO YOUR OWN STATE CONSTITUTION *and lastly,* THE ADDITIONAL SECURITY WHICH ITS ADOPTION WILL AFFORD TO THE PRESERVATION OF THAT SPECIES OF GOVERNMENT, TO LIBERTY, AND TO PROPERTY.

MODERN version of FEDERALIST # 1

unclear or misleading. I shall not, however, say much more about this. My motives must remain hidden in my own heart. My arguments, however, will be open to all and may be judged by all. They will be offered in a spirit of truthfulness that we all seek.

[10]I propose in this series, The Federalist Papers, to discuss the following details: the usefulness of this Union of American States for the improvement of your political life; the inability of the present government under the Articles of Confederation to maintain a united country; the necessity of having a government at least as strong and active as the one proposed by the new Constitution in order to ensure the survival of a Union of the States; the faithfulness of the proposed Constitution to the principles of republican government; how similar the proposed federal Constitution is to the constitution of the

ORIGINAL of FEDERALIST # 1

(11)In the progress of this discussion I shall endeavor to give a satisfactory answer to all the objections which shall have made their appearance, that may seem to have any claim to your attention.

(12)It may perhaps be thought superfluous to offer arguments to prove the utility of the UNION, a point, no doubt, deeply engraved on the hearts of the great body of the people in every State, and one, which it may be imagined, has no adversaries. But the fact is, that we already hear it whispered in the private circles of those who oppose the new Constitution, that the thirteen States are of too great extent for any general system, and that we must of necessity resort to separate confederacies

State of New York; and lastly, the additional protection that the new Constitution will give to the preservation of liberty, property, and a representative democracy.

[11]In the course of writing these papers, I will try to give a satisfactory answer to all objections that may cause you concern.

[12]It may seem unnecessary to offer arguments proving the usefulness of uniting the States into one country. Support for a union is, without a doubt, deeply engraved in the hearts of the great majority of the people in every state. And we might think that no one would be opposed to it. But, in fact, we already hear it whispered within the private circles of those who oppose the new Constitution that the thirteen States occupy too large a territory to be within one governmental system. They say we must resort to dividing the country into separate and

ORIGINAL of FEDERALIST # 1

of distinct portions of the whole.[2] *This doctrine will, in all probability, be gradually propagated, till it has votaries enough to countenance an open avowal of it. For nothing can be more evident, to those who are able to take an enlarged view of the subject, than the alternative of an adoption of the new Constitution or a dismemberment of the Union. It will therefore be of use to begin by examining the advantages of that Union, the certain evils, and the probable dangers, to which every State will be exposed from its dissolution. This shall accordingly constitute the subject of my next address.*

PUBLIUS

---

[2] We can find the same idea expressed in several of the recent publications against the new Constitution if we follow those arguments to their logical conclusions.

independent confederacies.[2] This belief will, in all probability, be gradually spread until it has enough supporters that they will be willing to publicly acknowledge it. To those who can see the bigger picture, nothing can be clearer than this: there are only two alternatives, to adopt the new Constitution or to break the Union apart. It will therefore be useful to begin this series of papers by examining the advantages of uniting the States, and to show the certain evils and probable dangers that every State will be exposed to if the Union is dissolved. My next essay shall, therefore, address this subject.

Friend of PUBLIUS

[2.] We can find the same idea expressed in several of the recent publications against the new Constitution if we follow those arguments to their logical conclusions.

RESEARCH AND DISCUSSION QUESTIONS for *Federalist #1*

1. In your opinion, is a strong and effective national government more of a threat or a guarantee of personal freedom?

2. What countries other than the U.S. have a federal form of government? What similarities shared by these countries make a federal form of government a logical choice for them?

3. What were the major objections of the Antifederalists to the new Constitution? Looking back over the last 200 years of U.S. history, do you think any of the Antifederalists' fears were realistic?

4. According to Thomas Jefferson, we should rewrite our Constitution every thirty years or so. If we were to rewrite it today, what changes should we make?

The Federal Procession was the first parade down Broadway in New York City. It began at around 10:00 AM at the sound of 13 guns, fired from the Federal Ship Hamilton. The Hamilton was a parade float complete in every detail honoring the New Yorker most responsible for the ratification of the Constitution.

Author's Introduction to

THE FEDERALIST #10
The Union as A Safeguard Against Domestic Faction and Insurrection
November 23, 1787

· ·

·

In this, James Madison's first contribution to The Federalist Papers, he deals with the influence of factions, a problem that many political thinkers then (as now) considered a major threat to democracy. By a faction, he means a group of people united by a common interest that is different from, and may conflict with, the national interest or the public good. Today we often call factions as special interest groups.

Although not directly addressed by Madison, at the heart of this discussion is the question of how to maximize the liberty of the individual – which would include the freedom to pursue one's own self-interest – while protecting the order and stability of society.

As Madison looked back over the history of democracies, he saw that many had failed because of what we would now call "the problem of special interest groups." He opens this essay with the assertion that the American governments of his time, which would have included the States' governments as well as the national government under The Articles of Confederation, were being destabilized by groups of people following their own, narrow self-interests. The cure for these problems, he argues, is either to eliminate factions or to control them.

He goes on to show that eliminating factions is inconsistent with the principles of democracy and impossible due to the nature of man. Therefore the only solution is to control factions, thereby limiting the harm that they can cause.

The question then becomes how best to control the effect of factions. He answers by showing that republics (democracies that elect representatives to govern them) are more capable of controlling factions than are pure democracies. In pure democracies (also called direct democracies), the voting public participates directly in law-making thereby giving existing factions the power to enact laws entirely for their own benefit. On the other hand, republics filter the will of the people through statesmen. These statesmen, he argues, will be elected because they have the nation's best interest at heart. This is the weakest part of Madison's argument. If there is a majority faction, then they have only to act together to elect a government official who will pass laws tailored to their own interest in order to succeed.

Madison goes on, however, to explain that the size of the proposed union of thirteen states would comprise a sufficiently large territory so that a majority faction would be unlikely to emerge. The faction that arose in support of The Revolutionary War against England, and, indeed the faction that arose in support of a new constitution to replace The Articles, calls this assertion into question. It may be fairly noted that James Madison was, in fact, a prominent member of both of those factions.

Nevertheless, *Federalist #10* is especially relevant to the problems faced by the country today. Some would say that the problem of campaign finance reform--the power of "dark money"--is really about the ability of special interest groups to distort the political process. Law-makers who attempt to pass laws in the areas of public health and safety, climate change, voting rights, gun control, reproductive rights, to name a few, face highly polarized public opinions. These opinions have in many cases been shaped by the influence of special interest groups.

In the first part of *Federalist #10*, Madison analyzes the causes and effects of factions. For Madison, "factions" included political parties as well as special interest groups. However, our modern political parties might not be included because they are each composed of many different factions. Madison's definition of "a faction" may not accurately describe them.

In the second part of the essay, he goes on to explain how the new government proposed by the Constitution of 1787 provides solutions to the problem of factions.

Terms to know before you read the essay: (see Glossary)

- Interest groups
- Factions, Factious
- Republics
- Divisiveness
- Pure (Direct) Democracy
- Legislation
- Democracy
- Majority
- Minority
- Public Good

GUIDED READING QUESTIONS for
Students to answer as you read

1. How does Madison justify his concerns about the problem of factions?

2. Why is it impractical and unwise to eliminate factions?

3. What aspects of human nature make factions inevitable?

4. How does the existence of factions undermine law-making?

5. Why are majority-factions more dangerous to democracy than minority-factions?

6. Why are pure democracies more vulnerable to factions than republics (representative democracies)?

7. What are two important differences between a pure democracy and a republic?

8. Why are good representatives more likely to be elected in a large republic than in a small republic?

9. Why does a small republic need more representatives in proportion to its population than a larger republic?

10. Why is a smaller republic less likely to find enough good representatives?

11. Why are majority-factions more likely to form in a small republic than a large one?

ORIGINAL of *Federalist #10*

[1]AMONG the numerous advantages promised by a well constructed Union, none deserves to be more accurately developed than its tendency to break and control the violence of faction. The friend of popular governments never finds himself so much alarmed for their character and fate, as when he contemplates their propensity to this dangerous vice. He will not fail, therefore, to set a due value on any plan which, without violating the principles to which he is attached, provides a proper cure for it.

[2]The instability, injustice, and confusion introduced into the public councils, have, in truth, been the mortal diseases under which popular governments have everywhere perished; as they continue to be the favorite and fruitful topics from which the adversaries to liberty derive their most specious declamations. The valuable improvements made by the American constitutions on the popular models, both ancient and

<u>MODERN</u> *version of Federalist #10*

[1]THERE are many advantages to be gained by having a well-constructed government for the United States. Furthermore, no advantage is more important, none more deserving of careful explanation, than the ability of such a government to weaken and control the negative effects of factions. Those who support democracy are most alarmed that this type of government is particularly susceptible to the problem of factions. Friends of democracy will therefore greatly value a plan that cures this dangerous tendency without violating republican principles.

[2]In truth, popular governments have failed in the past because they have succumbed to instability, injustice and confusion. The enemies of freedom continue to use these problems to incorrectly argue that democratic republics cannot succeed. Even though the constitutions of the states as well as the Articles of Confederation deserve to be greatly

ORIGINAL of FEDERALIST # 10

modern, cannot certainly be too much admired; but it would be an unwarrantable partiality, to contend that they have as effectually obviated the danger on this side, as was wished and expected. Complaints are everywhere heard from our most considerate and virtuous citizens, equally the friends of public and private faith, and of public and personal liberty, that our governments are too unstable, that the public good is disregarded in the conflicts of rival parties, and that measures are too often decided, not according to the rules of justice and the rights of the minor party, but by the superior force of an interested and overbearing majority.

[3]However anxiously we may wish that these complaints had no foundation, the evidence, of known facts will not permit us to deny that they are in some degree true. It will be found, indeed, on a candid review of our situation, that some of the distresses under which

MODERN version of FEDERALIST # 10

admired for the improvements they make to the basic models of democracy, both ancient and modern, it would be a mistake to assume that they have completely eliminated the problem of special interests. Many of our most thoughtful and upstanding citizens, true and faithful to the cause of liberty in their public as well as their private lives, complain that our governments have been too unstable. They contend that the public good is forgotten in the struggles between special interest groups. Judgments are not made according to the rules of justice and the rights of those in the minority but according to the interests of a forceful majority.

[3]Although we wish that these things were not so, the available facts force us to admit that to some extent they are true. Judging our situation honestly, we must say that we have wrongly blamed our governments for some of our problems, but others

ORIGINAL of FEDERALIST # 10

we labor have been erroneously charged on the labor have been erroneously charged on the operation of our governments; but it will be found, at the same time, that other causes will not alone account for many of our heaviest misfortunes; and, particularly, for that prevailing and increasing distrust of public engagements, and alarm for private rights, which are echoed from one end of the continent to the other. These must be chiefly, if not wholly, effects of the unsteadiness and injustice with which a factious spirit has tainted our public administrations.

[4]By a faction, I understand a number of citizens, whether amounting to a majority or a minority of the whole, who are united and actuated by some common impulse of passion, or of interest, adverse to the rights of other citizens, or to the permanent and aggregate interests of the community.

MODERN version of FEDERALIST # 10

--some of our worst problems—cannot truthfully be blamed on anything else but our government. This is particularly true of the public's increasing distrust in our governing institutions and their fearfulness about the safety of individual rights. One hears these concerns repeated throughout the country. These problems must primarily be due to the instability and injustice, which the divisiveness of factions has caused in our governments.

[4]By a faction, I mean a group of citizens, whether a majority or minority of the whole, who are united and motivated by a common interest or deeply held belief, which may conflict with the rights of other citizens or with the permanent, collective interests of the community.

ORIGINAL of FEDERALIST # 10

(5)*There are two methods of curing the mischiefs of faction: the one, by removing its causes; the other, by controlling its effects.*

(6)*There are again two methods of removing the causes of faction: the one, by destroying the liberty which is essential to its existence; the other, by giving to every citizen the same opinions, the same passions, and the same interests.*

(7)*It could never be more truly said than of the first remedy, that it was worse than the disease. Liberty is to faction what air is to fire, an aliment without which it instantly expires. But it could not be less folly to abolish liberty, which is essential to political life, because it nourishes faction, than it would be to wish the annihilation of air, which is essential to animal life, because it imparts to fire its destructive agency.*

(8)*The second expedient is as impracticable as the first would be unwise. As long as the reason of man*

MODERN version of FEDERALIST # 10

(5)There are two methods of curing the negative effects of faction: the first is by removing the causes of factions; the other, by controlling its effects.

(6)There are again two methods of removing the causes of faction: the one, by destroying the freedom that is essential to its existence; the other, by giving to every citizen the same opinions, the same passions (deeply held beliefs), and the same interests.

(7)Certainly it is true that the first remedy is worse than the disease it would cure. Freedom is to faction what air is to fire, an element without which it instantly dies. But it is as foolish to abolish freedom because it nourishes faction as it would be to abolish air because it feeds the destructive power of fire.

(8)The second solution is as impractical as the first is unwise. As long as human reasoning is

ORIGINAL of FEDERALIST # 10

continues fallible, and he is at liberty to exercise it, different opinions will be formed. As long as the connection subsists between his reason and his self-love, his opinions and his passions will have a reciprocal influence on each other; and the former will be objects to which the latter will attach themselves. The diversity in the faculties of men, from which the rights of property originate, is not less an insuperable obstacle to a uniformity of interests.

[9]The protection of these faculties is the first object of government. From the protection of different and unequal faculties of acquiring property, the possession of different degrees and kinds of property immediately results; and from the influence of these on the sentiments and views of the respective proprietors, ensues a division of the society into different interests and parties.

MODERN version of FEDERALIST # 10

imperfect, and men have the freedom to put their ideas into action, they will form opinions. As long as there is a connection between reasoning and self-interest, each will influence the other, and self-interest will attach itself to rational ideas. The right of private property, originating in our different skills and abilities, also prevents people from having the same interests.

[(9)]The protection of these individual abilities is the primary function of government. As a result of having different talents, people will possess different kinds and different amounts of property. The possession of different property will influence the thinking and the beliefs of its owners so that society will inevitably be divided into different interest groups and parties.

ORIGINAL of FEDERALIST # 10

(10)The latent causes of faction are thus sown in the nature of man; and we see them everywhere brought into different degrees of activity, according to the different circumstances of civil society.   A zeal for different opinions concerning religion, concerning government, and many other points, as well of speculation as of practice; an attachment to different leaders ambitiously contending for pre-eminence and power; or to persons of other descriptions whose fortunes have been interesting to the human passions, have, in turn, divided mankind into parties, inflamed them with mutual animosity, and rendered them much more disposed to vex and oppress each other than to co-operate for their common good.

(11)So strong is this propensity of mankind to fall into mutual animosities, that where no substantial occasion presents itself, the most frivolous and fanciful distinctions have been sufficient to kindle their unfriendly passions and excite their most violent conflicts.

MODERN version of FEDERALIST # 10

[10]Hence, the hidden causes of factions are contained within human nature and their appearance depends on the form of government within which they exist. Mankind has been divided into different parties by an enthusiasm for different opinions about religion or government, or by loyalty to different political leaders. Or, they are divided by their loyalty to those who have captured the public's imagination.

[11]A love of argument has inflamed men with mutual animosity and made them more likely to annoy and oppress each other than to work together for some common good. Man has a great capacity for hatred and therefore even the smallest and most unimportant differences have been enough to produce anger and violence.

ORIGINAL of FEDERALIST # 10

(12)But the most common and durable source of factions has been the various and unequal distribution of property. Those who hold and those who are without property have ever formed distinct interests in society. Those who are creditors, and those who are debtors, fall under a like discrimination. A landed interest, a manufacturing interest, a mercantile interest, a moneyed interest, with many lesser interests, grow up of necessity in civilized nations, and divide them into different classes, actuated by different sentiments and views. The regulation of these various and interfering interests forms the principal task of modern legislation, and involves the spirit of party and faction in the necessary and ordinary operations of the government.

MODERN version of FEDERALIST # 10

[12]But the strongest and most common source of faction has been the unequal distribution of various kinds of wealth. Those who have wealth have always been motivated by interests that are different from the interests of those who are not wealthy, like creditors and debtors. Groups composed of wealthy landowners, manufacturers, merchants, bankers and financiers, etc., are a necessary part of a civilized nation. However they will divide that nation into different classes, activated by different opinions and perspectives. The principle task of modern legislation is to regulate these conflicting and aggressive interests. Therefore, government will necessarily become involved with political parties and factions.

ORIGINAL of FEDERALIST # 10

(13)*No man is allowed to be a judge in his own cause, because his interest would certainly bias his judgment, and, not improbably, corrupt his integrity. With equal, nay with greater reason, a body of men are unfit to be both judges and parties at the same time; yet what are many of the most important acts of legislation, but so many judicial determinations, not indeed concerning the rights of single persons, but concerning the rights of large bodies of citizens? And what are the different classes of legislators but advocates and parties to the causes which they determine? Is a law proposed concerning private debts? It is a question to which the creditors are parties on one side and the debtors on the other.*

(14)*Justice ought to hold the balance between them. Yet the parties are, and must be, themselves the judges; and the most numerous party, or, in other words, the most powerful faction must be expected to prevail. Shall*

MODERN version of FEDERALIST # 10

[13]No man is allowed to be a judge in his own case because his self-interest would certainly bias his judgment and also, probably, corrupt his integrity. With equal or greater reason, groups of people are also unfit to be both the judge and the defendant in the same case. Yet, many of the most important laws are nothing more than judgments, not about the rights of single individuals but about the rights of large groups of citizens. And what are the lawmakers but attorneys and defendants in the cases about which they are making judgments? If a law is proposed concerning debts, the debtors are the defendants and the creditors are the plaintiffs.

[14]Justice ought to hold the balance between them. Yet, the two opposing groups must also be the judges. The most numerous party--the most powerful faction--will probably win. Shall U.S. manufacturers be protected from foreign competition by restrictions on imports? And if they

domestic manufactures be encouraged, and in what degree, by restrictions on foreign manufactures? are questions which would be differently decided by the landed and the manufacturing classes, and probably by neither with a sole regard to justice and the public good. The apportionment of taxes on the various descriptions of property is an act which seems to require the most exact impartiality; yet there is, perhaps, no legislative act in which greater opportunity and temptation are given to a predominant party to trample on the rules of justice. Every shilling with which they overburden the inferior number, is a shilling saved to their own pockets.

[15]It is in vain to say that enlightened statesmen will be able to adjust these clashing interests, and render them all subservient to the public good. Enlightened statesmen will not always be at the helm. Nor, in many cases, can such an adjustment be made at all without taking into view indirect and remote considerations, which will rarely

are, how much protection should they receive? These are questions that would be answered differently by the manufacturing class rather than by the wealthy landowners, and neither would answer the questions only according to what is just and in the public's interest. Making laws about how much tax will be paid on various kinds of property requires a keen sense of fairness and neutrality. Yet, there is perhaps no act of legislation that gives greater opportunity for powerful interests to trample on the rules of justice. Every penny by which they can overtax another group is a penny more in their own pocket.

[15]It is useless to say that enlightened statesmen will be able to mediate these conflicting interests and make them all serves the needs of the public. Enlightened statesmen will not always be at the helm. Nor will it always be possible to carefully craft a law, weighing all the indirect and remote

THE FEDERALIST PAPERS: A Modern Translation in Parallel Text

ORIGINAL of FEDERALIST # 10

prevail over the immediate interest which one party may find in disregarding the rights of another or the good of the whole.

(16)The inference to which we are brought is, that the CAUSES of faction cannot be removed, and that relief is only to be sought in the means of controlling its EFFECTS.

(17)If a faction consists of less than a majority, relief is supplied by the republican principle, which enables the majority to defeat its sinister views by regular vote. It may clog the administration, it may convulse the society; but it will be unable to execute and mask its violence under the forms of the Constitution. When a majority is included in a faction, the form of popular government, on the other hand, enables it to sacrifice to its ruling passion or interest both the public good and the

effects it is likely to have, when one group might immediately get an advantage over the rights of another group or even the rights of the public from the passage of the law.

[16]We must conclude that the CAUSES of faction cannot be eliminated and that the solution is, therefore, to control its EFFECTS.

[17]If a faction consists of less than a majority, the solution is provided by democracy itself, which allows the majority to defeat the minority's sinister view by voting against it. The minority may be able to slow down the government in the exercise of its duties, it may be able to disrupt society, but it will be unable to disguise and carry out its violence within a Constitutional framework of government. On the other hand, when the majority forms a faction, democratic rule enables the majority to sacrifice the public good and the rights of the minority to its own interests or beliefs. The

ORIGINAL of FEDERALIST # 10

rights of other citizens. To secure the public good and private rights against the danger of such a faction, and at the same time to preserve the spirit and the form of popular government, is then the great object to which our inquiries are directed. Let me add that it is the great desideratum by which this form of government can be rescued from the opprobrium under which it has so long labored, and be recommended to the esteem and adoption of mankind.

(18)By what means is this object attainable? Evidently by one of two only. Either the existence of the same passion or interest in a majority at the same time must be prevented, or the majority, having such coexistent passion or interest, must be rendered, by their number and local situation, unable to concert and carry into effect schemes of oppression. If the impulse and the

MODERN version of FEDERALIST # 10

question these essays (The Federalist Papers) attempt to answer is how we can protect the public good and individual rights against the danger of a majority faction, and at the same time preserve the ideals and the organization of a democracy. Solving the problem of a tyrannizing majority is the critical task that must be accomplished if we are to rescue the democratic form of government from the contempt with which it has been held. We would then be able to honorably recommend it as worthy to be adopted for our use.

[18]How will we attain this goal? Evidently, only by one of two ways: either we must prevent the same passion or interest from being held by a majority of individuals at the same time, or we must find a way to prevent this majority from organizing

ORIGINAL of FEDERALIST # 10

opportunity be suffered to coincide, we well know that neither moral nor religious motives can be relied on as an adequate control. They are not found to be such on the injustice and violence of individuals, and lose their efficacy in proportion to the number combined together, that is, in proportion as their efficacy becomes needful.

[19]From this view of the subject it may be concluded that a pure democracy, by which I mean a society consisting of a small number of citizens, who assemble and administer the government in person, can admit of no cure for the mischiefs of faction. A common passion or interest will, in almost every case, be felt by a majority of the whole; a communication and concert result from the form of government itself; and there is nothing to check the inducements to sacrifice the weaker party or an obnoxious individual. Hence it is that such democracies have ever been spectacles of turbulence and contention; have ever been found incompatible with

and carrying out their schemes of oppression. If the intention and the opportunity to act on it are allowed to coincide, we know that neither a sense of morality or religious belief can be relied on as an adequate control. We know that they often do not work on an individual level to stop injustice and violence. We also know that their ability to control human behavior diminishes as the number of people in the group increases. That is to say, the more restraint is needed, the less morals or religion will be able to provide that restraint.

[19]From this point of view, we may conclude that a governmental cure for harmful factions cannot be found in a pure democracy. By a pure democracy, I mean a society consisting of a small number of citizens, who assemble and administer the government in person. A common passion or interest will, in almost every case, be held by a majority of the whole. Their ability to organize and

ORIGINAL of FEDERALIST # 10

personal security or the rights of property; such democracies have ever been spectacles of turbulence and contention; have ever been found incompatible with personal security or the rights of property; and have in general been as short in their lives as they have been violent in their deaths. Theoretic politicians, who have patronized this species of government, have erroneously supposed that by reducing mankind to a perfect equality in their political rights, they would, at the same time, be perfectly equalized and assimilated in their possessions, their opinions, and their passions.

[20]A republic, by which I mean a government in which the scheme of representation takes place, opens a different prospect, and promises the cure for which we are seeking. Let us examine the points in which it varies from pure democracy, and we shall comprehend both the nature of the cure and the efficacy which it must derive from the Union.

act collectively is provided by the form of government itself. And, there is nothing to counteract their motivation to sacrifice the rights of the weaker party or the unpopular individual. It is for this reason that pure democracies have always been spectacles of instability and bickering. They have always proven to be incompatible with personal safety and the rights of property. They have in general been as short in their lives as they have been violent in their deaths. Political thinkers who have recommended pure democracy, mistakenly suppose that when men are granted political equality, they will also become equal in their possessions, their opinions, and their passions.

[20]A republic, by which I mean a representative democracy, is substantially different and does offer the cure to faction that we are seeking. Let us examine the points in which a representative democracy (a republic) differs from a pure

ORIGINAL of FEDERALIST # 10

(21)The two great points of difference between a democracy and a republic are: first, the delegation of the government, in the latter, to a small number

of citizens elected by the rest; secondly, the greater number of citizens, and greater sphere of country, over which the latter may be extended.

(22)The effect of the first difference is, on the one hand, to refine and enlarge the public views, by passing them through the medium of a chosen body of citizens, whose wisdom may best discern the true interest of their country, and whose patriotism and love of justice will be least likely to sacrifice it to temporary or partial considerations. Under such a regulation, it may well happen that the public voice, pronounced by the representatives of the people, will be more consonant to the public good than if pronounced by the people themselves, convened for the purpose.

democracy, and we will understand both the nature of the cure and the effectiveness that the cure derives from the type of government proposed by the new Constitution.

[21]There are two great points of difference between a pure democracy and a republic. Firstly, a small number of people elected by the rest run the government in a republic. Secondly, a republic may extend over a greater number of citizens and a larger territory than may a pure democracy

[22]The effect of the first difference is that public opinion will be refined and made more enlightened by first being passed through the medium of a chosen body of citizens who will wisely understand the true interests of their country. These representatives' patriotism and love of justice will make them less likely to sacrifice the interests of the country in favor of a temporary passion or local interest. Under republican rule it may well happen

ORIGINAL of FEDERALIST # 10

(23)*On the other hand, the effect may be inverted. Men of factious tempers, of local prejudices, or of sinister designs, may, by intrigue, by corruption, or by other means, first obtain the suffrages, and then betray the interests, of the people. The question resulting is, whether small or extensive republics are more favorable to the election of proper guardians of the public weal; and it is clearly decided in favor of the latter by two obvious considerations:*

(24)*In the first place, it is to be remarked that, however small the republic may be, the representatives must be raised to a certain number, in order to guard against the cabals of a few; and that, however large it may be, they must be limited to a certain number, in* that the public's voice pronounced by its representatives will be more attuned to the public good than it would have been if pronounced by the people themselves in a pure democracy.

[23]On the other hand, representative democracy may have the opposite effect. Men who do not think of the common good, nor of the national interest, or who have bad intentions may, by trickery or bribery or other means, first obtain the votes and then betray the interests of the people. The question we must ask is whether good representatives who will protect the well being of the nation are more likely to be elected in a small or a large republic. The answer is clearly that good representatives are more likely in a large republic for two reasons.

[24]In the first place we should point out that however small the republic, the number of representatives must be great enough so that a few

ORIGINAL of FEDERALIST # 10

order to guard against the confusion of a multitude. Hence, the number of representatives in the two cases not being in proportion to that of the two constituents, and being proportionally greater in the small republic, it follows that, if the proportion of fit characters be not less in the large than in the small republic, the former will present a greater option, and consequently a greater probability of a fit choice.

(25)In the next place, as each representative will be chosen by a greater number of citizens in the large than in the small republic, it will be more difficult for unworthy candidates to practice with success the vicious arts by which elections are too often carried; and the suffrages of the people being more free, will be more likely to centre in men who possess the most attractive merit and the most diffusive and established characters.

can not conspire successfully to take over. And, yet, the number should be small enough so that government can proceed in an efficient and orderly manner. Therefore, the proportion of the number of representatives to the number of citizens will not necessarily be the same in a small and a large republic. A small republic will need to have more representatives compared to the size of its population than will a large republic. If we assume that the proportion of people who would make good representatives is about the same in any population, we must conclude that it will be harder to find enough good candidates in a smaller republic than in a larger republic.

[25]Also, because each representative will be chosen by a greater number of people in a large republic, it will be more difficult for unworthy candidates to win by unfair practices and trickery. In addition, men of merit, whose good character is

ORIGINAL of FEDERALIST # 10

(26)It must be confessed that in this, as in most other cases, there is a mean, on both sides of which inconveniences will be found to lie. By enlarging too much the number of electors, you render the representatives too little acquainted with all their local circumstances and lesser interests; as by reducing it too much, you render him unduly attached to these, and too little fit to comprehend and pursue great and national objects. The federal Constitution forms a happy combination in this respect; the great and aggregate interests being referred to the national, the local and particular to the State legislatures.

well and widely known are more likely to be elected because voting will be less affected by unfair campaigning.

[26]It must be confessed that in this, as in most things, a happy medium exists on both sides of which inconveniences lie. By enlarging the number of representatives too much, we will cause them to be too little aware of the concerns and interests of the people and locations they represent. By reducing the number of representatives, we will cause them to be too much attached to their local and special interests and less able to understand and pursue great or national goals. The federal Constitution creates a happy combination in this respect. The great and general interests are referred to the national Congress while the local and particular are handled by the State legislatures. The great and general interests are referred to the

ORIGINAL of FEDERALIST # 10

(27)*The other point of difference is, the greater number of citizens and extent of territory which may be brought within the compass of republican than of democratic government; and it is this circumstance principally which renders factious combinations less to be dreaded in the former than in the latter.*

(28)*The smaller the society, the fewer probably will be the distinct parties and interests composing it; the fewer the distinct parties and interests, the more frequently will a majority be found of the same party; and the smaller the number of individuals composing a majority, and the smaller the compass within which they are placed, the more easily will they concert and execute their plans of oppression.* (29)*Extend the sphere, and you take in a greater variety of parties and interests; you make it less probable that a majority of the whole will have a common motive*

national Congress while the local and particular are handled by the State legislatures.

[27]The other point of difference is the greater number of citizens and the larger extent of territory that can be governed under a representative democracy rather than a pure democracy. This difference is the primary reason that factions are less to be feared in large republics than in small ones.

[28]The smaller the society, the fewer different parties and interests that will exist, and the more likely it will be that one of these factions will contain a majority of the citizens. Furthermore, the smaller the number of people required to form a majority faction, and the smaller the territory they wish to control, the easier it will be for them to organize and carry out their schemes of oppression.

[29]In a larger republic, there is a greater variety of parties and interests. It is less likely that there will

ORIGINAL of FEDERALIST # 10

to invade the rights of other citizens; or if such a common motive exists, it will be more difficult for all who feel it to discover their own strength, and to act in unison with each other. Besides other impediments, it may be remarked that, where there is a consciousness of unjust or dishonorable purposes, communication is always checked by distrust in proportion to the number whose concurrence is necessary.

(30)Hence, it clearly appears, that the same advantage which a republic has over a democracy, in controlling the effects of faction, is enjoyed by a large over a small republic, is enjoyed by the Union over the States composing it. Does the advantage consist in the substitution of representatives whose enlightened views and virtuous sentiments render them superior to local prejudices and schemes of injustice?

ever be a common motive among a majority of thecitizens to invade the rights of others, or if a common motive did exist, it would be more difficult for all who feel it to recognize that they are a majority and the more difficult it will be for so many people to act in unison. Besides other obstacles to overcome, when people have an unjust or dishonorable purpose their distrustfulness makes it difficult for them to communicate with each other. The greater number of people involved, the greater their distrustfulness will be.

[30]Hence, it clearly appears that the same advantage that a republic has over a pure democracy, a large republic also has over a small republic. Therefore, the union of American States has these advantages over the individual States that compose it. Does this advantage exist because enlightened and virtuous federal representatives will

ORIGINAL of FEDERALIST # 10

(31)It will not be denied that the representation of the Union will be most likely to possess these requisite endowments. Does it consist in the greater security afforded by a greater variety of parties, against the event of any one party being able to outnumber and oppress the rest? In an equal degree does the increased variety of parties comprised within the Union, increase this security. Does it, in fine, consist in the greater obstacles opposed to the concert and accomplishment of the secret wishes of an unjust and interested majority? Here, again, the extent of the Union gives it the most palpable advantage.

(32)The influence of factious leaders may kindle a flame within their particular States, but will be unable to spread a general conflagration through the other States. A religious sect may degenerate into a political faction in a part of the Confederacy; but the variety of sects dispersed over the entire face of it must secure the

MODERN version of FEDERALIST # 10

be above local and narrow self-interests and schemes of injustice?

[31]It will not be denied that representatives of the Union will be most likely to possess those required qualities. Does the Union have this advantage because in its large expanse there will be a greater variety of parties and interests and less likelihood that any of them will be large or powerful enough to outnumber or oppress the rest? Finally do its advantages result from the greater obstacles which would prevent an unjust and self-interested majority from organizing and accomplishing its secret wishes? Here again the size of the Union gives it the most apparent advantage.

[32]The influence of factious leaders may kindle a flame within their particular State but will be unable to spread a larger fire through the other States. A religious sect may degenerate into a political faction

ORIGINAL of FEDERALIST # 10

national councils against any danger from that source. A rage for paper money, for an abolition of debts, for an equal division of property, or for any other improper or wicked project, will be less apt to pervade the whole body of the Union than a particular member of it; in the same proportion as such a malady is more likely to taint a particular county or district, than an entire State.

[33]In the extent and proper structure of the Union, therefore, we behold a republican remedy for the diseases most incident to republican government. And according to the degree of pleasure and pride we feel in being republicans, ought to be our zeal in cherishing the spirit and supporting the character of Federalists.

PUBLIUS

in one part of the country, but the variety of religions found throughout the nation will prevent harm to the Union from political groups based on a particular religious sect. A demand for over-printing money, for abolishing debts, for the equal distribution of wealth, or for any other improper or wicked scheme will be less likely to affect the whole country than of a particular part of it. In the same way, these problems are more likely to infect a particular county or district than an entire State.

[33]In the size and organization of the Union under the new Constitution, therefore, we find a republican remedy for the diseases most common to democratic government. We should cherish the ideals of federalism and support its unique features to the same extent that we feel pride and pleasure in our belief in a republican form of government.

Friend of PUBLIUS

RESEARCH AND DISCUSSION QUESTIONS for *Federalist #10*

1. What is Madison's view of human nature? Do you agree with him? Why or why not?

2. How did the framers of the Constitution feel about political parties? Would Madison view our modern political parties as factions?

3. List three to four groups that you consider factions. Explain why each one would fit Madison's definition.

4. What effects did <u>Citizens United v. FEC</u> (2010) have on the ability of special interest groups to influence elections?

Author's Introduction to

THE FEDERALIST #39
The Conformity of the Plan to Republican Principles
January 17, 1788

. . . .

.

In *Federalist #39*, James Madison addresses the primary objection to the Constitution--the belief that the new national government would effectively eliminate the power and sovereignty of the states. The opponents of the Constitution were not eager for the states to relinquish the independence they had fought the British to establish and that they felt had been secure under the Articles of Confederation. Those who supported stronger state governments, the Antifederalists, felt that because each state had its own particular economic base, its own customs, and its own interests, each should be able to make laws tailored to fit its particular circumstances without interference.

Furthermore, since 1783 there had been conflict between several adjoining states arising from boundary disputes, trade barriers, and over-printed currency. As a result, they were not predisposed to trust each other in a stronger union nor did they trust the powerful national government proposed by the Constitution of 1787. On the other side, the Federalists believed a stronger union was required to protect the young country from instability from within and aggression from without.

Madison attempts in this essay to allay the fears of the Antifederalists, or at least to deprive them of an argument, and to secure the support of the undecided. He describes the new government as a finely crafted compromise between a confederal government and a highly centralized unitary, national government. This compromise government would balance the prerogatives of local government against the necessity for unity and strength.

Unitary governments are characterized by a strong central authority that grants limited sovereignty to local governments. An example would be the government of the United Kingdom. Confederal governments are the opposite. They are characterized by having strong, independent local governments that empower a weak central government to carry out some functions that they cannot perform as well on their own. There are few existing examples of confederacies due to the instability of this form of government. The United Nations is a confederal organization, as was the U.S. under the Articles of Confederation, and the Confederate States of America (CSA) during the Civil War.

A federal government is a hybrid mix of the first two. It consists of strong states or local governments as well as a strong central government, both the local and central governments being sovereign within their own spheres of power. Typically the central government has authority over issues such as national security whereas the local governments have authority over law and order within their own territories. This form of government was first formally attempted under the U.S. Constitution of 1787 and has since been adopted by other large, diverse nations such as Mexico, India, Canada and Australia.

Federalist #39 opens with a discussion of the requirements of true representation. In a true republic, the people elect or appoint all government officials, whether directly by voting for them or indirectly through the choices made by those they do elect. Terms of office must either be for some specified amount of time or indefinite but with the possibility of the official being fired or impeached. Madison defines a true republic by these criteria and shows that the new government is a true republic. He then attends to the more serious charges, that the proposed government is a return to the highly centralized government that had been rejected along with British rule, and that it represents an abandonment of self-government and local sovereignty. He answers that the new government is a careful balance of unitary and confederal features.

The method of ratification chosen for the new Constitution is confederal in that the states must ratify it and not a majority of the people as a whole. No state can be forced to join the union just because a majority of other states has voted to join. The sovereignty of each state is therefore preserved. Proportional representation based on population in the House of Representatives, is a unitary feature of the new government.

The Senate, on the other hand, which is based on equal representation (two senators) from each state, is a confederal institution. In the election of the president through the Electoral College, there are elements of both forms of government.

The laws of the national government will apply directly to the citizens, not indirectly to them through the states. In this way the government is unitary.

However, the separation of powers between the state governments and the national government, creating different spheres within which each is sovereign, he identifies as a confederal feature. And finally the process of amending the Constitution partakes of both forms of government. Three-fourths of the states must ratify (a confederal feature) but any dissenting states are bound by the vote of the majority (a unitary feature).

Madison begins this essay by showing how the terms of office under the new Constitution are based on those of the states, and he ends by detailing the many provisions of the Constitution that allow the states to continue the co-equal and independent status they have enjoyed under the Articles of Confederation. Modeled on the states and incorporating their sovereignty, he asserts that the new government is neither radical nor dangerous.

He only briefly admits that the national government is in a superior position in this new arrangement when he says that disputes between a state and the federal government will be decided in a national (federal) court. He then dismisses this as a source of conflict by asserting, without proof, that the federal judiciary will be impartial in these disputes. It is interesting to consider John Marshall's decisions in <u>Gibbons v. Ogden</u> (1819) and <u>McCulloch v. Maryland</u> (1824) in light of this assertion.

In fact, the subsequent history of federalism shows an enlargement of the powers of the federal government at the expense of state powers justified by the Supreme Court's interpretation of the Supremacy Clause, the Necessary and Proper Clause and the Interstate Commerce Clause. None of these is mentioned in *Federalist #39.*

The Constitution, in fact, seems to have created the conditions for a power struggle that several times has threatened to tear the nation apart and once erupted into a civil war. On the other hand, even though the intricate balance between two separate spheres of power painstakingly constructed in the Constitution has not survived the intervening two hundred plus years perfectly intact, the federal republic, which that document created, has. The success of this hybrid government is further attested to by the other large democracies that have successfully adopted its form.

Terms to know before you read the essay: (see Glossary)

- Unitary governments
- Confederal governments
- Federal governments
- Legislative branch
- Executive branch
- Judicial branch
- Ratification
- Popular Government
- Republic
- Impeachment
- Republican
- Sphere of power
- Elite
- Sovereignty

GUIDED READING QUESTIONS for Students to
answer as you read

1. What are two characteristics of a true republic?

2. The state governments were models for what aspects of the new national government?

3. The opponents of the new Constitution claimed that it did not create a true republic and that it was not close enough to what other form of government?

4. Does the procedure for ratification more closely resemble a unitary or a confederal process?

5. Does Congress represent a unitary or a confederal feature of the new government? Explain your answer.

6. How does the Electoral College combine elements of both unitary and confederal government?

7. Madison says that the laws of the new government will operate directly on the citizens, not on the citizens indirectly through the states. Does this make the government more unitary or confederal? Explain your answer.

8. How does the new Constitution allow for local matters to be decided at the local level and national matters to be decided at the national level?

9. How is the amendment process a combination of unitary and confederal features?

ORIGINAL *of Federalist #39*

(1)THE last paper having concluded the observations which were meant to introduce a candid survey of the plan of government reported by the convention, we now proceed to the execution of that part of our undertaking.

(2)The first question that offers itself is, whether the general form and aspect of the government be strictly republican. It is evident that no other form would be reconcilable with the genius of the people of America; with the fundamental principles of the Revolution; or with that honorable determination which animates every votary of freedom, to rest all our political experiments on the capacity of mankind for self-government. If the plan of the convention, therefore, be found to depart from the republican character, its advocates must abandon it as no longer defensible.

(3)What, then, are the distinctive characters of the republican form? Were an answer to this question to be

MODERN version of Federalist #39

(1)The *Federalist # 38* having concluded our introduction to the new Constitution, we can now examine the new government in detail.

(2)The first question we need to answer is whether the general form of the new government is strictly republican. Clearly, no other form would fit the special character of the American people, the basic principles of the Revolution, and the desire of all those who love freedom to base our political experiments on the capacity of mankind for self-government. If the new Constitution, therefore, departs from the principle of republican government, its advocates cannot honorably defend it.

(3)Then what characterizes a republican form of government? If we look at the way political writers use the term in describing the constitutions of different governments, we will not find a satisfactory answer. The whole world calls Holland

ORIGINAL of FEDERALIST # 39

sought, not by recurring to principles, but in the application of the term by political writers, to the constitution of different States, no satisfactory one would ever be found. Holland, in which no particle of the supreme authority is derived from the people, has passed almost universally under the denomination of a republic. The same title has been bestowed on Venice, where absolute power over the great body of the people is exercised, in the most absolute manner, by a small body of hereditary nobles. Poland, which is a mixture of aristocracy and of monarchy in their worst forms, has been dignified with the same appellation. The government of England, which has one republican branch only, combined with an hereditary aristocracy and monarchy, has, with equal impropriety, been frequently placed on the list of republics. These examples, which are nearly as dissimilar to each other as to a

a republic when no part of its government's powers is derived from the people. The same title has been given to the city-state of Venice where absolute power over the people is exercised by a hereditary ruling class. Poland, which is a mixture of aristocracy and monarchy in their most extreme forms has been honored with the same name--a republic. The government of England, which has only one republican (representative) branch, combined with a hereditary aristocracy and monarchy, has just as incorrectly been called a republic. These examples, which are as different from each other as they all are from a genuine republic, show how inaccurately the term "republic" is used in political writing.

genuine republic, show the extreme inaccuracy with which the term has been used in political disquisitions.

[4]*If we resort for a criterion to the different principles on which different forms of government are established, we may define a republic to be, or at least may bestow that name on, a government which derives all its powers directly or indirectly from the great body of the people, and is administered by persons holding their offices during pleasure, for a limited period, or during good behavior. It is essential to such a government that it be derived from the great body of the society, not from an inconsiderable proportion, or a favored class of it; otherwise a handful of tyrannical nobles, exercising their oppressions by a delegation of their powers, might aspire to the rank of republicans, and claim for their government the honorable title of republic.*

[4]By referring to the principles upon which governments are established, we may define a republic as a government that derives all of its powers directly or indirectly from the people, and is administered by officers who hold their positions for limited terms or for unlimited terms with the possibility of impeachment for improper conduct. It is essential that such a government derive its power from the people as a whole, not from a small faction or a favored class. Otherwise, a few members of an economic or political elite, oppressing the people through their appointed officials, might want to call themselves republicans and claim for their government the honorable title of a republic.

ORIGINAL of FEDERALIST # 39

(5)*It is sufficient for such a government that the persons administering it be appointed, either directly or indirectly, by the people; and that they hold their appointments by either of the tenures just specified; otherwise every government in the united states, as well as every other popular government that has been or can be well organized or well executed, would be degraded from the republican character. According to the constitution of every state in the union, some or other of the officers of government are appointed indirectly only by the people.*

(6)*According to most of them, the chief magistrate himself is so appointed. And according to one, this mode of appointment is extended to one of the co-ordinate branches of the legislature. According to all the constitutions, also, the tenure of the highest offices is extended to a definite period, and in many instances, both within the legislative and executive departments,*

MODERN version of FEDERALIST # 39

(5)To be called a republic, it is enough that the persons administering the government be directly or indirectly appointed by the people, and that they hold their appointments for a limited term or during a term of good behavior. Any other method of choosing an executive branch would undermine the principle of a government elected by the people, regardless of how well organized and well executed it might be.

(6)According to the constitutions of every state in the union, some officers are appointed indirectly by the people. According to most state constitutions, the governor is also appointed indirectly by the people. And according to one state constitution this method of choosing officials is also used for one of the branches of its legislature. According to all of these constitutions, also, all terms of office are for a specific, limited number of years. According to the provisions of most of the states'

ORIGINAL of FEDERALIST # 39

to a period of years. According to the provisions of most of the constitutions, again, as well as according to the most respectable and received opinions on the subject, the members of the judiciary department are to retain their offices by the firm tenure of good behavior.

(7)On comparing the Constitution planned by the convention with the standard here fixed, we perceive at once that it is, in the most rigid sense, conformable to it. The House of Representatives like that of one branch at least of all the State legislatures, is elected immediately by the great body of the people. The Senate, like the present Congress, and the Senate of Maryland, derives its appointment indirectly from the people.

(8)The President is indirectly derived from the choice of the people, according to the example in most of the States. Even the judges, with all other officers of the Union, will, as in the several States, be the choice, though a remote choice, of the people themselves, the

constitutions, and the most respected opinions on the subject, the judges are to retain their offices permanently with the possibility of impeachment for improper conduct.

(7)Comparing the standards set by the State constitutions to the proposal that we are examining here (the new Constitution), we see at once that the new Constitution strictly conforms to the standard set by the constitutions of the States. The House of Representatives is elected directly by the people in the new Constitution, the same as the lower house in each State legislature. The new Senate is appointed indirectly by the people, like the Senate under the Articles of Confederation and the Senate of the State of Maryland.

(8)The President is indirectly elected by the choice of the people in a manner that is similar to the selection of the governors of the States. As in the individual States, even judges and all other

appointments is equally conformable to the republican standard, and to the model of State constitutions.   The House of Representatives is periodically elective, as in all the States; and for the period of two years, as in the State of South Carolina.   The Senate is elective, for the period of six years; which is but one year more than the period of the Senate of Maryland, and but two more than that of the Senates of New York and Virginia.

(9)The President is to continue in office for the period of four years; as in New York and Delaware, the chief magistrate is elected for three years, and in South Carolina for two years.   In the other States the election is annual. In several of the States, however, no constitutional provision is made for the impeachment of the chief magistrate.   And in Delaware and Virginia he

Presidential appointments will be the choice, though very indirectly, of the people themselves. The terms of office also conform to the standard of republican governments and the model of the State constitutions. The House of Representatives is elected at regular intervals as in all the States and for the period of two years as in the State of South Carolina. The Senate is elected for a period of six years, which is only one year more than the Senate is elected for in the State of Maryland and only two more than are the Senates of New York and Virginia.

[9]The President is in office for a period of four years. The governors of New York and Delaware are elected for terms of three years and in South Carolina for two years. In other States the election is annual. In several of the States, however, no provision is made for the impeachment of the governor, and in Delaware and Virginia he is not

is not impeachable till out of office. The President of the United States is impeachable at any time during his continuance in office. The tenure by which the judges are to hold their places, is, as it unquestionably ought to be, that of good behavior. The tenure of the ministerial offices generally, will be a subject of legal regulation, conformably to the reason of the case and the example of the State constitutions.

(10)Could any further proof be required of the republican complexion of this system, the most decisive one might be found in its absolute prohibition of titles of nobility, both under the federal and the State governments; and in its express guaranty of the republican form to each of the latter.

(11)But it was not sufficient," say the adversaries of the proposed Constitution, "for the convention to adhere to the republican form. They ought, with equal care, to

impeachable until he is out of office. By contrast, the President of the United States is impeachable at any time during his term of office. The term of office for judges is, as it unquestionably ought to be, that of good behavior (that is, unlimited except in the case of impeachment). The term of office for executive branch officials other than the President will be decided by Congress according to the nature of the job that the official will do, and to the example of the State constitutions.

[10]Could any further proof be required that this is a republican government, the most decisive would be that the Constitution absolutely prohibits titles of nobility (this is quite as true for the national government as for the State governments), and guarantees a republican form of government for each of the States.

[11]But it isn't enough, say the opponents of the new Constitution, that the Framers chose a

THE FEDERALIST PAPERS: A Modern Translation in Parallel Text

ORIGINAL of FEDERALIST # 39

have preserved the FEDERAL form, which regards the Union as a CONFEDERACY of sovereign states; instead of which, they have framed a NATIONAL government, which regards the Union as a CONSOLIDATION of the States." And it is asked by what authority this bold and radical innovation was undertaken? The handle which has been made of this objection requires that it should be examined with some precision.

(12)Without inquiring into the accuracy of the distinction on which the objection is founded, it will be necessary to a just estimate of its force, first, to ascertain the real character of the government in question; secondly, to inquire how far the convention were authorized to propose such a government; and thirdly, how far the duty they owed to their country could supply any defect of regular authority.

republican form of government, they ought to have cared as much about establishing a confederal form of government, which would regard the Union as a confederacy of sovereign States. Instead of which they have formed a unitary national government that regards the Union as a consolidation of the States. They further ask by whose authority this bold and radical innovation was undertaken? We need to examine these objections carefully as they are often raised. [The first is examined in this paper and the second is examined in *Federalist No. 40.*]

[12]Whether or not we agree with this distinction between a confederacy of the States, on the one hand, and consolidation of the States on the other hand, to fairly judge the merits of this argument, we first need to find out what this new government is really like. Secondly, we need to ask if the delegates to Philadelphia were authorized to propose a new form of government. Thirdly, we should ask how

ORIGINAL of FEDERALIST # 39

(13)*First. In order to ascertain the real character of the government, it may be considered in relation to the foundation on which it is to be established;*

to the sources from which its ordinary powers are to be drawn; to the operation of those powers; to the extent of them; and to the authority by which future changes in the government are to be introduced.

(14)*On examining the first relation, it appears, on one hand, that the Constitution is to be founded on the assent and ratification of the people of America, given by deputies elected for the special purpose; but, on the other, that this assent and ratification is to be given by the people, not as individuals composing one entire nation, but as composing the distinct and independent States to which they respectively belong. It is to be the assent and ratification of the several States, derived from the supreme authority in each State, the authority of the*

much their sense of duty and devotion to their country can make up for any lack of authorization.

[13]First, in order to discover the real nature of the government, that is whether it is confederal or unitary, we need to look at how it will be ratified by the people; to the sources of its powers; to its use of those powers; to the scope of those powers; and to the source of authority by which this government can be changed.

[14]On examining the first point relating to the real nature of the government, it appears that the Constitution is to be founded on the approval of the people of America through their elected delegates to State ratifying conventions. However, this approval is to be given by the people not as individuals composing one nation but as individuals composing the distinct and independent States to which they belong. The approval of the States will be derived from the supreme authority of each

people themselves. The act, therefore, establishing the Constitution, will not be a NATIONAL, but a FEDERAL act.

(15)*That it will be a federal and not a national act, as these terms are understood by the objectors; the act of the people, as forming so many independent States, not as forming one aggregate nation, is obvious from this single consideration, that it is to result neither from the decision of a MAJORITY of the people of the Union, nor from that of a MAJORITY of the States. It must result from the UNANIMOUS assent of the several States that are parties to it, differing no otherwise from their ordinary assent than in its being expressed, not by the legislative authority, but by that of the people themselves.*

(16)*Were the people regarded in this transaction as forming one nation, the will of the majority of the whole people of the United States would bind the minority, in*

State, that is, from the authority of the people themselves. The act of establishing the Constitution will not be a unitary act (that is, the act of a nation of people), but a confederal act (that is, the act of an association of sovereign States).

[15]That the ratification will be confederal in nature is proven by this single fact: ratification will result not from the decision of a majority of the people in the Union nor from a majority of the States. It must result from the approval of every State that is to be a part of the new nation.

[16]If the people were looked upon as forming one nation, the ratification of the Constitution would only require a majority vote of the whole people of the United States. The majority approval would also obligate the dissenting minority. The will of the majority would be determined by a general vote of all the people or by the approval of a majority of all the States (which would also

the same manner as the majority in each State must bind the minority; and the will of the majority must be determined either by a comparison of the individual votes, or by considering the will of the majority of the States as evidence of the will of a majority of the people of the United States. Neither of these rules have been adopted. Each State, in ratifying the Constitution, is considered as a sovereign body, independent of all others, and only to be bound by its own voluntary act. In this relation, then, the new Constitution will, if established, be a FEDERAL, and not a NATIONAL constitution.

[17]*The next relation is, to the sources from which the ordinary powers of government are to be derived. The House of Representatives will derive its powers from the people of America; and the people will be represented in the same proportion, and on the same principle, as they are in the legislature of a particular State. So far the government is NATIONAL, not FEDERAL. The*

obligate the dissenting States). But neither of these rules has been adopted. Each State in ratifying the Constitution is considered sovereign and independent and can only obligate itself to the new government by its own voluntary act. Therefore, the new Constitution in its method of ratification will be confederal and not unitary.

[17]We can now look at the second point--the source from which the government derives its powers. The House of Representatives will derive its powers from the people of America and the people will be proportionally and directly represented just as they are in the representative house of their own State legislatures. So far then, the government is unitary and not confederal. The Senate, on the other hand will derive its powers from the States as political equals. They will be represented on the principle of equality in the Senate as they now are in the existing Continental

Senate, on the other hand, will derive its powers from the States, as political and coequal societies; and these will be represented on the principle of equality in the Senate, as they now are in the existing Congress. So far the government is FEDERAL, not NATIONAL.

(18)The executive power will be derived from a very compound source. The immediate election of the President is to be made by the States in their political characters. The votes allotted to them are in a compound ratio, which considers them partly as distinct and coequal societies, partly as unequal members of the same society.

Congress under the Articles of Confederation. So in this respect the government is confederal not unitary.

[18]The executive power will be derived from several sources. The first step in the election of the President is to be made by each State. By choosing some of the Electors in proportion to their populations, the States are looked upon as unequal because they are unequal in population. By choosing some Electors on the principle of equality, the States are looked upon as equally sovereign and important. The electors then will represent the will of the people in a way that is both unitary and confederal. Unitary because a certain number of electors are chosen according to the population of

(19)*The eventual election, again, is to be made by that branch of the legislature which consists of the national representatives; but in this particular act they are to be thrown into the form of individual delegations, from so many distinct and coequal bodies politic. From this aspect of the government it appears to be of a mixed character, presenting at least as many FEDERAL as NATIONAL features.*

MODERN version of FEDERALIST # 39

each State and therefore the people are represented equally as if they were the people of one nation even though the States are represented unequally. And a number of electors are also chosen on the confederal principle, that is, each State has the same two Electors as every other State.

[19]However, if no candidate receives a majority of Electoral votes, the election will be decided in the House of Representatives according to the Constitution. The House is the branch of Congress where the people are represented equally as though they were the people of one nation. Even though this is a unitary feature there is a confederal component as well because all the Representatives from a State will comprise the State delegation and together they will have one vote to cast in the election of the President. And so, even though representation is based on a unitary principle in the

ORIGINAL of FEDERALIST # 39

(20)The difference between a federal and national government, as it relates to the OPERATION OF THE GOVERNMENT, is supposed to consist in this, that in the former the powers operate on the political bodies composing the Confederacy, in their political capacities; in the latter, on the individual citizens composing the nation, in their individual capacities. On trying the Constitution by this criterion, it falls under the NATIONAL, not the FEDERAL character; though perhaps not so completely as has been understood.

(21)In several cases, and particularly in the trial of controversies to which States may be parties, they must be viewed and proceeded against in their collective and political capacities only. So far the national countenance of the government on this side seems to be disfigured by a few federal features. But this blemish is perhaps unavoidable in any plan; and the operation of the government

MODERN version of FEDERALIST # 39

House of Representatives, the method of election will be confederal. Again we see that the government from this point of view appears to be a mixture with as many confederal as unitary features.

[20]The difference between the way a confederal as opposed to a unitary government operates amounts to this, that in a confederal system the powers of the central government operate on the states composing a confederacy, while unitary governments operate on the individual citizens who compose the nation. Judging the Constitution by this standard, it falls under the unitary and not the confederal category, although perhaps not so completely as you may at first think.

[21]In some cases, particularly in settling disputes between the States, the powers of the national government must operate on the States. But in the ordinary operations of government, the people will be dealt with directly by the national

on the people, in their individual capacities, in its ordinary and most essential proceedings, may, on the whole, designate it, in this relation, a NATIONAL government.

(22)But if the government be national with regard to the OPERATION of its powers, it changes its aspect again when we contemplate it in relation to the EXTENT of its powers. The idea of a national government involves in it, not only an authority over the individual citizens, but an indefinite supremacy over all persons and things, so far as they are objects of lawful government. Among a people consolidated into one nation, this supremacy is completely vested in the national legislature. Among communities united for particular purposes, it is vested partly in the general and partly in the municipal legislatures. In the former case, all local authorities are subordinate to the supreme; and may be controlled, directed, or abolished by it at pleasure.

MODERN version of FEDERALIST # 39

government as individual citizens. So by the definition of the Antifederalists, it will be a unitary government.

[22]But if the government is unitary in respect to how it uses its powers, it seems to be more confederal when we consider the scope of those powers. A unitary government, compared to a confederal government, does not merely have authority over individual citizens but an absolute supremacy over all persons and things that are subject to any government control. In unitary governments this supremacy is held by a national legislature. In confederal nations, sovereignty is held partly by the national and partly by the local legislatures. In the case of a unitary form of government, all local units of government are subordinate to the central state government and canbe controlled, directed, or abolished by it at any time.

[23]*In the latter, the local or municipal authorities form distinct and independent portions of the supremacy, no more subject, within their respective spheres, to the general authority, than the general authority is subject to them, within its own sphere. In this relation, then, the proposed government cannot be deemed a NATIONAL one; since its jurisdiction extends to certain enumerated objects only, and leaves to the several States a residuary and inviolable sovereignty over all other objects. It is true that in controversies relating to the boundary between the two jurisdictions, the tribunal which is ultimately to decide, is to be established under the general government. But this does not change the principle of the case.*

MODERN version of FEDERALIST # 39

[23]In a confederal form, local government holds independent and sovereign power over those things that it has a right to control. Within the powers reserved to States by the Constitution, they are no more subject to the authority of the central government than the central government is subject to them within its own sphere of powers. And in this relationship of shared and independent sovereignty, the proposed government cannot really be called a unitary one since it has only a certain number of powers which are spelled out in the Constitution and it leaves to the States all other powers, powers that cannot be violated by the central government. It is true that when there is a dispute about the boundary between the federal government's and the States' spheres of power, the court that will ultimately decide the question is a court of the federal government and not of one of

ORIGINAL of FEDERALIST # 39

(24)*The decision is to be impartially made, according to the rules of the Constitution; and all the usual and most effectual precautions are taken to secure this impartiality. Some such tribunal is clearly essential to prevent an appeal to the sword and a dissolution of the compact; and that it ought to be established under the general rather than under the local governments, or, to speak more properly, that it could be safely established under the first alone, is a position not likely to be combated.*

(25)*If we try the Constitution by its last relation to the authority by which amendments are to be made, we find it neither wholly NATIONAL nor wholly FEDERAL. Were it wholly national, the supreme and ultimate authority would reside in the MAJORITY of the people of the Union; and this authority would be*

the States. However, this does not change the basic argument.

[24]The decision of that court is to be made impartially according to the rules of the Constitution with all the usual precautions taken to insure impartiality. Some court is clearly necessary to resolve disputes between the States otherwise they will resort to violence, which will lead to the dissolution of the whole Union. Furthermore, this court could only be safely established under the national government. It is obvious that only a national court would be regarded as impartial by the disputing States.

[25]If we try the Constitution by examining the authority by which amendments to the Constitution are to be made, we find that, again, the government will be neither completely unitary nor completely confederal. If it were unitary, the powers of the government would be derived by a majority vote of

ORIGINAL of FEDERALIST # 39

competent at all times, like that of a majority of every national society, to alter or abolish its established government.

(26)Were it wholly federal, on the other hand, the concurrence of each State in the Union would be essential to every alteration that would be binding on all.

(27)The mode provided by the plan of the convention is not founded on either of these principles. In requiring more than a majority, and particularly in computing the proportion by STATES, not by CITIZENS, it departs from the NATIONAL and advances towards the FEDERAL character; in rendering the concurrence of less than the whole number of States sufficient, it loses again the FEDERAL and partakes of the NATIONAL character.

all the people. This authority would be enough to amend or even to abolish the government.

[26]If the new government were completely confederal, on the other hand, the approval of each State in the Union would be essential to ratify an amendment that would be binding on all the States.

[27]Instead, the method provided by the new Constitution does not depend on either of these principles alone. First, it requires more than a simple majority, it requires a three-fourths majority and that is three-fourths not of the citizens but of the States. In this respect, it is less unitary and more confederal in character. And, in allowing an amendment to pass by less than a unanimous vote of the States, it loses the pure confederal form and comes closer to the unitary form.

THE FEDERALIST PAPERS: A Modern Translation in Parallel Text

ORIGINAL of FEDERALIST # 39

(28)The proposed Constitution, therefore, is, in strictness, neither a national nor a federal Constitution, but a composition of both. In its foundation it is federal, not national; in the sources from which the ordinary powers of the government are drawn, it is partly federal and partly national; in the operation of these powers, it is national, not federal; in the extent of them, again, it is federal, not national; and, finally, in the authoritative mode of introducing amendments, it is neither wholly federal nor wholly national.

PUBLIUS

[28]The proposed Constitution, therefore, even when tested by the rules laid down by the Antifederalists is strictly speaking neither a unitary nor a confederal Constitution but a combination of both. In its method of ratification, it is not unitary but confederal. In the source from which the government derives its power, it is partly confederal and partly unitary. In the exercise of these powers it is unitary not confederal. In the scope of these powers it is confederal not unitary. And finally, in the way it is to be amended it is neither wholly confederal nor completely unitary.

Friend of PUBLIUS

RESEARCH AND DISCUSSION QUESTIONS for *Federalist #39*

1. How does Madison attempt to convince the public that the new government under the Constitution will not be radical or dangerous?

2. What were the objections of the Antifederalists? In what ways has subsequent history proved them right or wrong?

3. Do the modern powers of the national government make policy-making more or less difficult?

4. How have the following historical events tipped the balance of power between the federal and the state governments?

- the emergence of big business after the Civil War
- the Great Depression
- the Cold War
- the Civil Rights Movement

5. Which level of government holds the most power today? Explain

Author's Introduction to

THE FEDERALIST #51

The Structure of the Government Must Furnish the Proper Checks and Balances Between the Different Departments

February 8, 1788

....

In *The Federalist Papers #49-50* James Madison argued that no <u>external</u> control--neither the people as a whole nor a specially appointed council of censors--would be adequate to prevent the abuse of power by those in government. In this essay, he describes how the <u>internal</u> framework of the Constitution would minimize the opportunities of those in government to overstep their legitimate authority.

In the *Federalist #51*, Madison eloquently writes about the general problem of creating and maintaining a just government: "...you must first enable the government to control the governed; and in the next place oblige it to control itself."

Governments are always a balance between the power of the government and liberty of the individual. The specific question Madison addresses in *Federalist #51* is, How will the proposed Constitution protect our liberty from the abuse of those who hold political power? In *Federalist #10* he concentrated on the problem of factions taking over the government and ruling for their own benefit, ignoring or violating the rights of other citizens. Part of the Constitutional protection against the problem of faction is a government of carefully defined powers separated among three branches. A faction may manage to dominate one of the states but not all the states, one branch of government but not all three branches of government simultaneously.

In this essay, Madison continues the general lines of this discussion, adding that a system of checks and balances is necessary to further prevent one branch of the government from becoming a tyrannical force. Each branch is to be as independent from the other two as is practical, and each is to possess the ability and the motivation to prevent the others from taking over total control of the government. At the end of this essay he returns to the problem of factions declaring that a large republic with many diverse groups is less susceptible to the problems of factions. The United States under the proposed Constitution would be such a republic, combining the benefits of diversity with the protection of separate branches as well as checks and balances.

The principle of separation of powers was widely accepted in 1787. Establishing a satisfactory balance of power among those branches and maintaining the independence of each of these while requiring them to work together constituted the real problem. As colonies, the Americans had experience with overbearing executives in the form of colonial governors who sometimes ruled arbitrarily, overriding the decisions of representative assemblies, thwarting the will of the governed and subverting the powers of government for their own benefit.

When the states were free to establish their own governments, many chose the opposite arrangement of power, weak executives and strong legislatures. Indeed this was the case with the national government under the Articles of Confederation during this time as well. The lack of a strong executive under the Articles caused government to be ineffectual. Weak and dependent judicial branches were not protected from political pressures. For example, judges salaries were sometimes withheld or adjusted in order to pressure them to rule in favor of the majority in the majority of elected officials in the State's legislative assembly.

As Edmund Randolph said during the Philadelphia Convention, "Our chief danger arises from the democratic parts of our constitutions. It is a maxim which I hold incontrovertible, that the powers of government exercised by the people swallows up the other branches." Although Madison does not address it as such, many modern commentators consider the checks and balances established in the Constitution as being inspired by the anti-majoritarian, anti-democratic sentiment shared by most of the men who wrote the Constitution.

Although the combination of separation of powers and checks and balances seems to have served us well over the subsequent history of the country, it has also produced significant problems. The independent decisions of the Supreme Court have sometimes run counter to the will of the people. This was the case with the Court's ruling against the progressive legislation during the 1920s and the early New Deal legislation in the 1930s. It is the case today in such controversial areas as prayer in school and reproductive rights. In the modern era of a government divided between two political parties as well as separated into three branches, important problems such as voting rights, immigration reform, growing inequality, climate change, and health care may go unresolved.

Terms to know before you read the essay: (see Glossary)

- legislative
- judicial
- executive
- the Philadelphia Convention
- liberty
- private sector
- to check (verb)
- republican government
- unitary government

- federal republic
- faction
- majority
- minority
- sects
- factious

GUIDED READING QUESTIONS for Students to
answer as you read

1. Why will judicial branch officials (judges and justices) remain politically independent even though they are appointed by the executive and approved by the legislature?

2. If Congress could raise or lower the President's salary, it would be difficult for him to remain independent. Why?

3. What two groups must government control?

4. For what purpose is power distributed in governments, or in any organization?

5. How will the powers of the legislative branch be balanced against those of the weaker, executive branch?

6. What features of the new Constitution doubly protect the rights of the people?

7. By what two methods can the rights of the minority be protected against the unjust actions of the majority?

8. What's wrong with creating a power independent of the voters whose job would be to protect minority interests?

9. Why, according to Madison, are rights less safe in a small republic than in a larger one?

10. When the rights of the minority are not protected, what eventually happens to the government?

11. What special features of the country and of the proposed government will protect the U.S. from the problems that usually plague republics?

George Washington used this chair for nearly three months as he presided over the Constitutional Convention. Benjamin Franklin is credited with immortalizing the chair at the close of the convention, observing: " I have often in the course of the summer, and my hopes and fears about the outcome, looked at the back of the chair behind the president without being able to tell whether it was a sunrise or sunset: But now, I have the happiness to know that it is a rising and not a setting Sun."

ORIGINAL *of Federalist # 51*

[(1)]TO WHAT expedient, then, shall we finally resort, for maintaining in practice the necessary partition of power among the several departments, as laid down in the Constitution? The only answer that can be given is, that as all these exterior provisions are found to be inadequate, the defect must be supplied, by so contriving the interior structure of the government as that its several constituent parts may, by their mutual relations, be the means of keeping each other in their proper places. Without presuming to undertake a full development of this important idea, I will hazard a few general observations, which may perhaps place it in a clearer light, and enable us to form a more correct judgment of the principles and structure of the government planned by the convention.

[(2)]In order to lay a due foundation for that separate and distinct exercise of the different powers of government, which to a certain extent is admitted on all

<u>MODERN</u> version of Federalist #51

(1)How shall we actually accomplish the separation of powers among the branches of government that the Constitution has established in theory? The answer is, that all exterior controls are inadequate. Organizing the government so that each branch will control the others through their relationships with each other must solve the problem. Without taking the time now to fully discuss this important idea, I will attempt a few general observations. These may clarify the issue as well as allow us to judge more correctly the principles and structure of the new government proposed at the Philadelphia Convention.

(2)It is generally agreed that a separation of powers among the branches of government is essential for the preservation of liberty. In order to base the exercise of separate powers on a solid foundation, it is clear that each branch should be

ORIGINAL of FEDERALIST # 51

hands to be essential to the preservation of liberty, it is evident that each department should have a will of its own; and consequently should be so constituted that the members of each should have as little agency as possible in the appointment of the members of the others. We see this principle rigorously adhered to, it would require that all the appointments for the supreme executive, legislative, and judiciary magistracies should be drawn from the same fountain of authority, the people, through channels having no communication whatever with one another.

(3)Perhaps such a plan of constructing the several departments would be less difficult in practice than it may in contemplation appear. Some difficulties, however, and some additional expense would attend the execution of it. Some deviations, therefore, from the principle must be admitted. In the constitution of the judiciary

able to act on its own. Consequently, each branch should be constructed so that it will have as little involvement as possible in selecting the representatives of the other branches. Were we to abide strictly by this principle, it would be necessary for the President, members of Congress, and the judges and justices of the judicial branch to be chosen by the people, who are the ultimate source of the government's power.

[3]Furthermore, the election process of each branch should be completely separated from the other two. Perhaps this would be less difficult than it sounds, although some difficulties and some additional expense would occur. Some deviations, therefore, from the strict principle of separate elections must be allowed. In the organization of the judicial branch, in particular, a strictly separate selection process would not be practical or necessary. Firstly, we must choose a method of

department in particular, it might be inexpedient to insist rigorously on the principle: first, because peculiar qualifications being essential in the members, the primary consideration ought to be to select that mode of choice which best secures these qualifications; secondly, because the permanent tenure by which the appointments are held in that department, must soon destroy all sense of dependence on the authority conferring them.

(4)It is equally evident, that the members of each department should be as little dependent as possible on those of the others, for the emoluments annexed to their offices. Were the executive magistrate, or the judges, not independent of the legislature in this particular, their independence in every other would be merely nominal.

(5)But the great security against a gradual concentration of the several powers in the same department, consists in giving to those who administer each department the necessary constitutional means and

selecting the members of this branch so that those who possess specific and special qualifications will most likely be found. Secondly, members of the judicial branch will quickly become very independent of those who selected them because they are appointed for life and can only be impeached for serious offenses.

[4]It is equally evident that members of each branch of government should depend as little as possible on members of the other branches for their pay. Were the President or the judges dependent on Congress for their pay, their independence in any other way would not be likely.

[5]But the best safeguard against the concentration of power in one branch is to give the members of each branch the constitutional means to stop the other branches from taking over its powers. The means of defense must in this case, as in all others, be equal to the danger of the attack.

personal motives to resist encroachments of the others. The provision for defense must in this, as in all other cases, be made commensurate to the danger of attack. Ambition must be made to counteract ambition. The interest of the man must be connected with the constitutional rights of the place. It may be a reflection on human nature, that such devices should be necessary to control the abuses of government. But what is government itself, but the greatest of all reflections on human nature? If men were angels, no government would be necessary.

(6)*If angels were to govern men, neither external nor internal controls on government would be necessary. In framing a government which is to be administered by men over men, the great difficulty lies in this: you must first enable the government to control the governed; and*

MODERN version of FEDERALIST # 51

Ambition must be made to counteract ambition. The self-interest of the person holding the office must be connected with the constitutional rights of that office. It may be a comment on human nature that such precautions should be necessary to control the abuse of government. But what is government itself but the greatest of all reflections on human nature.

[6]If men were angels, no government would be necessary. If angels were to govern men, no external nor internal controls on government would be necessary. In creating a government which is to be administered by men who will govern over other men, the great difficulty is this: you must first enable the government to control the governed and then oblige it to control itself. The vote of the people is the primary check on the powers of government, but experience has taught us that extra precautions are necessary.

ORIGINAL of FEDERALIST # 51

in the next place oblige it to control itself. A dependence on the people is, no doubt, the primary control on the government; but experience has taught mankind the necessity of auxiliary precautions.

(7)This policy of supplying, by opposite and rival interests, the defect of better motives, might be traced through the whole system of human affairs, private as well as public. We see it particularly displayed in all the subordinate distributions of power, where the constant aim is to divide and arrange the several offices in such a manner as that each may be a check on the other that the private interest of every individual may be a sentinel over the public rights. These inventions of prudence cannot be less requisite in the distribution of the supreme powers of the State.

(8)But it is not possible to give to each department an equal power of self-defense. In republican government,

MODERN version of FEDERALIST # 51

[7]This policy of making up for the absence of better motives by pitting interest against interest, can be seen throughout the whole system of human affairs, in the private sector as well as in government. We see it especially in the distribution of power within a command structure where the constant goal is to divide and arrange the many offices in such a way that each may be a check on the other. In other words, power should be arranged so that the self-interest of every individual will also become a guardian of the rights of the public. This careful distribution of power cannot be less important for the highest powers of a nation.

[8]But it is not possible to give to each branch an equal power of self-defense. In a republican government, the legislature will necessarily predominate. The solution to this problem is to divide Congress into two parts. Then it is necessary

ORIGINAL of FEDERALIST #51

the legislative authority necessarily predominates. The remedy for this inconveniency is to divide the legislature into different branches; and to render them, by different modes of election and different principles of action, as little connected with each other as the nature of their common functions and their common dependence on the society will admit. It may even be necessary to guard against dangerous encroachments by still further precautions.

(9)As the weight of the legislative authority requires that it should be thus divided, the weakness of the executive may require, on the other hand, that it should be fortified. An absolute negative on the legislature appears, at first view, to be the natural defense with which the executive magistrate should be armed. But perhaps it would be neither altogether safe nor alone sufficient. On ordinary occasions it might not be exerted with the requisite firmness, and on extraordinary

MODERN version of FEDERALIST # 51

to make the method of election and the power to act of these two parts as different as they possibly may be considering that the two parts have common functions and that they both derive their powers from the people. It may even be necessary to take further precautions to guard against one part of the government taking over another part.

[9]As the strength of the Congress requires that it must be divided, the weakness of the executive (the Presidency) may require, on the other hand, that it be fortified. The power to veto the legislature appears at first sight to be the natural defense with which the President should be armed. But, perhaps, it would not be altogether safe nor, by itself, sufficient. On ordinary occasions Presidents may not use the veto as forcefully as they should. In unusual circumstances, it may be used excessively and in ways that violate the public's trust. Perhaps

ORIGINAL of FEDERALIST # 51

occasions it might be perfidiously abused. May not this defect of an absolute negative be supplied by some qualified connection between this weaker department and the weaker branch of the stronger department, by which the latter may be led to support the constitutional rights of the former, without being too much detached from the rights of its own department?

(10)*If the principles on which these observations are founded be just, as I persuade myself they are, and they be applied as a criterion to the several State constitutions, and to the federal Constitution it will be found that if the latter does not perfectly correspond with them, the former are infinitely less able to bear such a test.*

(11)*There are, moreover, two considerations particularly applicable to the federal system of America, which place that system in a very interesting point of view.*

MODERN version of FEDERALIST # 51

this defect in the power of the veto can be corrected by creating a connection between the President and the Senate. By doing this, Congress may be led to support the Constitutional rights of the executive branch while still supporting and defending its own rights

(10)If the assumptions I have made are justified, and I believe they are, and if they are used to judge the State constitutions as well as the federal Constitution, we will see that the States meet this test far less well than does the new national government.

(11)There are, moreover, two aspects of the federal system we should look at which will show that proposed government in a favorable light.

ORIGINAL of FEDERALIST # 51

(12)*First. In a single republic, all the power surrendered by the people is submitted to the administration of a single government; and the usurpations are guarded against by a division of the government into distinct and separate departments. In the compound republic of America, the power surrendered by the people is first divided between two distinct governments, and then the portion allotted to each subdivided among distinct and separate departments. Hence a double security arises to the rights of the people. The different governments will control each other, at the same time that each will be controlled by itself.*

(13)*Second. It is of great importance in a republic not only to guard the society against the oppression of its rulers, but to guard one part of the society against the injustice of the other part. Different interests necessarily exist in different classes of citizens. If a majority be*

MODERN version of FEDERALIST # 51

[12]First, in a unitary government all the power surrendered by the people is given to a single, central government. Abuse of authority is prevented by dividing the powers of government into different branches. On the other hand, in the compound republic of America the power surrendered by the people is first divided between the States and the federal (national) government, and then subdivided into separate and distinct branches. Hence the rights of the people are doubly protected. The different governments will control each other, at the same time that each will be controlled by itself.

[13]Second, it is very important in a republic not only to guard society against the oppression of its rulers, but to guard one part of the society against the injustice of the other part. Different interests necessarily exist in different classes of citizens. If a majority be united by a common

ORIGINAL of FEDERALIST # 51

united by a common interest, the rights of the minority will be insecure. There are but two methods of providing against this evil: the one by creating a will in the community independent of the majority that is, of the society itself; the other, by comprehending in the society so many separate descriptions of citizens as will render an unjust combination of a majority of the whole very improbable, if not impracticable. The first method prevails in all governments possessing an hereditary or self-appointed authority. This, at best, is but a precarious security; because a power independent of the society may as well espouse the unjust views of the major, as the rightful interests of the minor party, and may possibly be turned against both parties.

[14]The second method will be exemplified in the federal republic of the United States. Whilst all authority in it will be derived from and dependent on the society, the society itself will be broken into so many parts,

MODERN version of FEDERALIST # 51

interest, the rights of the minority will not be safe. There are only two ways of preventing this evil: One is by creating a power in society independent of the majority. The other way is by creating a society with so many different classes of citizens that it would become improbable and impractical for a majority faction to exist. The first method of protecting the minority exists in all governments where power and authority is either hereditary (as in a monarchy) or self-appointed (as in a dictatorship). At best, this is flimsy security. A power not elected by the people may just as likely support the unjust views of the majority as the rightful views of the minority, or may turn against both.

[14]The second method of protecting minority rights can be seen in the federal republic of the United States. While all power and authority will come from the people, society itself will be divided into so many different parts, interests and classes of

interests, and classes of citizens, that the rights of individuals, or of the minority, will be in little danger from interested combinations of the majority. In a free government the security for civil rights must be the same as that for religious rights. It consists in the one case in the multiplicity of interests, and in the other in the multiplicity of sects.

(15)The degree of security in both cases will depend on the number of interests and sects; and this may be presumed to depend on the extent of country and number of people comprehended under the same government. This view of the subject must particularly recommend a proper federal system to all the sincere and considerate friends of republican government, since it shows that in exact proportion as the territory of the Union may be formed into more circumscribed Confederacies, or States oppressive combinations of a majority will be facilitated: the best security, under the republican forms, for the citizens, that the rights of the individual or of the minority will be in little danger from a majority. In a free society, civil rights must be as safe as religious rights. The safety of civil rights will be secured by the multiplicity of interests, the safety of religious rights by the multiplicity of sects.

[15]How secure civil or religious rights will be depends on the number of interests or the number of sects, and this number, we can assume, will depend on the size of the territory and the population of the country. Taking these arguments into account, a federal system must appeal to all sincere and thoughtful friends of a republican government. If the territory is divided into smaller republics, the formation of oppressive majorities will be made easier and the rights of every class of

rights of every class of citizens, will be diminished: and consequently the stability and independence of some member of the government, the only other security, must be proportionately increased.

(16)*Justice is the end of government. It is the end of civil society. It ever has been and ever will be pursued until it be obtained, or until liberty be lost in the pursuit. In a society under the forms of which the stronger faction can readily unite and oppress the weaker, anarchy may as truly be said to reign as in a state of nature, where the weaker individual is not secured against the violence of the stronger; and as, in the latter state, even the stronger individuals are prompted, by the uncertainty of their condition, to submit to a government which may protect the weak as well as themselves; so, in the former state, will the more powerful factions or parties be gradually induced, by a like motive, to wish for a government*

citizens will be endangered. Consequently the power of some independent authority -- the only other security -- must be proportionately increased.

[16]Justice is the goal of government. It is the goal of civil society. Justice has been and always will be pursued until it is obtained or until freedom has been lost in the process. Anarchy surely reigns under a government in which a majority faction may unite and oppress the minority, as much as it does where there is no government and where the weaker individual is not safe against the violence of the stronger. Where anarchy exists, even stronger individuals will be insecure and motivated to submit to a government that will protect the weaker members as well as themselves. So, also, will the more powerful factions or parties be gradually motivated to call for a government that will protect all parties, the weaker as well as the more powerful.

ORIGINAL of FEDERALIST #51

which will protect all parties, the weaker as well as the more powerful.

[17]It can be little doubted that if the State of Rhode Island was separated from the Confederacy and left to itself, the insecurity of rights under the popular form of government within such narrow limits would be displayed by such reiterated oppressions of factious majorities that some power altogether independent of the people would soon be called for by the voice of the very factions whose misrule had proved the necessity of it.

[18]In the extended republic of the United States, and among the great variety of interests, parties, and sects which it embraces, a coalition of a majority of the whole society could seldom take place on any other principles than those of justice and the *general good; whilst there being thus less danger to a minor from the will of a major party, there must be less pretext, also,*

[17]Undoubtedly, if the State of Rhode Island were separated from the rest of the country and left to itself, the repeated attacks of majority factions would cause rights to become so insecure that these same factions would call on an unelected and independent force to restore order.

[18]In the larger republic of the United States with its great variety of interests, parties and sects, an interest common to a majority of the citizens would rarely be found except for a general interest in justice and in the common good. Since there will be little need to protect minority rights against the ill-will of a majority, there won't be an excuse to empower an authority which is independent of the will of the majority of the people.

THE FEDERALIST PAPERS: A Modern Translation in Parallel Text

ORIGINAL of FEDERALIST # 51

to provide for the security of the former, by introducing into the government a will not dependent on the latter, or, in other words, a will independent of the society itself.

[19]It is no less certain than it is important, notwithstanding the contrary opinions which have been entertained, that the larger the society, provided it lie within a practical sphere, the more duly capable it will be of self-government. And happily for the REPUBLICAN CAUSE, the practicable sphere may be carried to a very great extent, by a judicious modification and mixture of the FEDERAL PRINCIPLE.

PUBLIUS

MODERN version of FEDERALIST # 51

[19]Contrary to criticisms which have been made, it is equally certain and important that the larger the country, the more capable it will be of self-government. Admittedly a country may be so large that self-government will be impractical. But happily for the republican cause, a very large self-governing country is practical if we adopt a wise modification and mixture of governments with divided powers.

Friend of PUBLIUS

RESEARCH AND DISCUSSION
QUESTIONS for *Federalist # 51*

1. How does our system of separated powers compare to a parliamentary system? Which system is more efficient? Which is more representative of the people it serves?

2. Madison says, "But what is government itself but the greatest reflection on human nature." Judging from the *Federalist #51* and from the structure of the government created by the Constitution of 1787, what is Madison's view of human nature?

3. In the *Federalist #51*, Madison expresses a view of human nature common in the late 18th century. How does that view compare to our modern view?

4. To many thinkers of the Enlightenment, human nature was perfectible. Institutions, like governments, should be constructed to improve the people they served. Did the Constitution of 1787 establish such a government?

5. Does the great diversity of the American people make the freedom of the individual more or less safe?

At the conclusion of the Constitutional Convention, Benjamin Franklin was asked what kind of government they had created, "A republic," he replied, "if you can keep it."

Author's Introduction to

THE FEDERALIST #53
The Same Subject Continued
(The House of Representatives)
February 12, 1788

The subject of Federalist #53 seems to be the rather narrow question of whether members of the House of Representatives should serve terms of two years, as proposed by the new Constitution of 1787, or one year as they had under the Articles of Confederation (1781-88). However, this essay like many of the other Federalist Papers, is really about limiting the powers of the national government while ensuring that it was strong enough to be effective.

A government of unlimited powers would be very effective and efficient. An absolute monarch would give a command and it would be carried out. Clearly however, the rights and liberties of the people could not be guaranteed under this system. At the other extreme, people would, theoretically at least, have immense freedom under a weak government of very limited powers, but that government would have great difficulty passing laws and enforcing them.

By 1788, there was a growing consensus in the States that the powers of the national government under the Articles of Confederation were too limited. The Continental Congress had been unable to pass much-needed legislation, to enforce its edicts, to maintain a sufficient national defense, or to put the new nation on a sound financial basis. Opinion was divided, however, on how to fix the problem.

Most thoughtful observers believed that the powers of the national government had to be strengthened; how much they should be strengthened was the question.

In this essay, Madison is arguing that the House of Representatives -- the only part of the government then directly elected by the voters -- should be given two-year terms. Under the Articles of Confederation, Congressional terms had been one year. Madison is attempting to refute the arguments of those who believed that extending Congressional terms would help to make this new far-away government too powerful.

To appreciate how remote and removed from their lives a central government would have seemed to those living in 1788, it is helpful to measure distance in travelling time. To get from one part of the U.S. to another could easily require two to four weeks of travel. Cities on the coast or villages on navigable rivers could communicate more easily. For those living inland, however, the roads were few and in the winter or rainy seasons could be washed out or become otherwise impassible. By comparison, few places on earth today are as distant in terms of travel time as was Albany, New York and rural Georgia in 1788. We can go to the moon and back in less time than that trip required. A national capital could seem as far away to them as the moon seems to us.

How long could a representative of the people live in a place far removed from them before he began to lose touch, to identify more with those he was engaged with on a daily basis? How could citizens hope to know what their representative was doing in a place so far away? How could they hold him accountable if at the end of the year, they could not replace him with someone else? If they could not hold their representative to account, how could they be sure he would not become corrupt, subordinating the rights of the people to his own interests and ambitions? Some of these questions are historically specific to 1788. Others are timeless or at least relevant to the current public debate over term limits.

Although term limits are often proposed simply for the calculated, if short-sighted, purpose of unseating incumbents of the opposite party, unbiased proponents see term limits as a means of diminishing the impact of money and special interests and of encouraging the citizen-legislator as opposed to the professional politician. In making a final judgment, it is useful to consider the experience of states and local governments, which have instituted term limits.   As with many reforms, the unintended negative consequences have often equaled or exceeded the benefits. Here is Madison's view.

Terms to know before you read the essay: (see Glossary)

- Tyranny
- Proverb
- Annual
- Term of office
- State assembly
- Legislator
- Constitution
- Parliament
- Unlimited government
- To legislate
- Legislation
- Commerce
- International law
- Legislature

GUIDED READING QUESTIONS for Students to

answer as you read

1. What arguments does Madison use to show that annual elections are not necessary?

2. What is he trying to prove when he compares the length of terms of various State governments?

3. What has the British parliament done that should alarm those who believe in free government?

4. Even though the U.S. under the new Constitution will not have elections every year, Madison argues that liberties will still be safer here than in other countries that do have annual elections. Why does he say this is so?

5. According to Madison, why is a one year term of office enough for a state legislator, but a two-year term necessary for a federal legislator?

6. Why should the size of a country affect the terms of office of its representatives?

7. Why does Madison predict that the U.S. will become easier to govern once the new Constitution is adopted?

8. Why do the challenges of foreign policy make longer terms more important?

9. Why should we consider the travel and living

arrangements that Representative must make when we are debating longer or shorter terms of office?

10. Why can't we compare the proposed terms of office to those of the Continental Congress under the Articles of Confederation?

11. In what ways will long-serving members of the House help newer members?

12. Why do shorter terms of office increase the likelihood that some people will try to get elected by dishonest means?

[1]*I SHALL here, perhaps, be reminded of a current observation, "that where annual elections end, tyranny begins." If it be true, as has often been remarked, that sayings which become proverbial are generally founded in reason, it is not less true, that when once established, they are often applied to cases to which the reason of them does not extend. I need not look for a proof beyond the case before us. What is the reason on which this proverbial observation is founded?*

[2]*No man will subject himself to the ridicule of pretending that any natural connection subsists between the sun or the seasons, and the period within which human virtue can bear the temptations of power. Happily for mankind, liberty is not, in this respect, confined to any single point of time; but lies within extremes, which afford sufficient latitude for all the variations which may be required by the various situations and circumstances of civil society. The*

MODERN version of Federalist #53

[1]I am reminded of a saying that is currently popular: "where annual elections end, tyranny begins." Many people believe that there is a grain of truth in every proverb. If this is so, then it is also true that proverbs are often applied to situations where they are not relevant. The case before us is a good example. What is the grain of truth in the proverb concerning annual elections?

[2]No one will be foolish enough to argue that there is a natural connection between the sun and seasons on the one hand and, on the other hand, the length of time that human virtue can resist the temptations of power. Happily for mankind, there is not a specific amount of time during which elected officials can be trusted with the powers of office, but a range of time which is wide enough to accommodate all of the needs of a nation. If it were appropriate, as it actually has been in some cases, officials might be elected for a period of a day, a

election of magistrates might be, if it were found expedient, as in some instances it actually has been, daily, weekly, or monthly, as well as annual; and if circumstances may require a deviation from the rule on one side, why not also on the other side? Turning our attention to the periods established among ourselves, for the election of the most numerous branches of the State legislatures, we find them by no means coinciding any more in this instance, than in the elections of other civil magistrates.

[3]*In Connecticut and Rhode Island, the periods are half-yearly. In the other States, South Carolina excepted, they are annual. In South Carolina they are biennial as is proposed in the federal government. Here is a difference, as four to one, between the longest and shortest periods; and yet it would be not easy to show, that Connecticut or Rhode Island is better governed, or enjoys a greater share of rational liberty, than South*

week or a month, as well as a year. And if circumstances sometimes may require a shorter term of office, why not a longer one? Turning to the example of State legislatures, we find many differences between the legislators' terms of office in various states, just as there are many differences between the lengths of terms for other state-level officials.

[3]In Connecticut and Rhode Island, State representatives are elected every six months. In all the other States except South Carolina, elections are yearly. South Carolina elects State representatives for two-year terms, as will be the case for the House of Representatives of the proposed federal government. South Carolina's terms of office are four times longer than Connecticut's or Rhode Island's. And, yet, it would be very hard to prove that Connecticut and Rhode Island with the shortest terms are better governed, or more orderly

Carolina; or that either the one or the other of these States is distinguished in these respects, and by these causes, from the States whose elections are different from both.

(4)In searching for the grounds of this doctrine, I can discover but one, and that is wholly inapplicable to our case. The important distinction so well understood in America, between a Constitution established by the people and unalterable by the government, and a law established by the government and alterable by the government, seems to have been little understood and less observed in any other country. Wherever the supreme power of legislation has resided, has been supposed to reside also a full power to change the form of the government. Even in Great Britain, where the principles of political and civil liberty have been most discussed, and where we hear most of the rights of the Constitution, it is maintained that the authority of the Parliament is

democracies than is South Carolina, which has the longest term. It would be equally hard to show that Connecticut, Rhode Island and South Carolina have either better or worse governments than those States that have neither the longest nor the shortest terms.

[4]In searching for the grain of truth in the argument for short terms of office, I have found just one, and that one is irrelevant to our case. However, there is a difference between a Constitution put in place by the people, which the elected government cannot alter, and a law passed by that government, which the government itself can alter. This distinction is well understood in America and little understood and less well practiced in other countries. In those places, it is assumed that the supreme legislative body also holds the power to alter the form of government. Which is to say, the government may on its own

ORIGINAL of FEDERALIST # 53

transcendent and uncontrollable, as well with regard to the Constitution, as the ordinary objects of legislative provision. They have accordingly, in several instances, actually changed, by legislative acts, some of the most fundamental articles of the government.

(5)They have in particular, on several occasions, changed the period of election; and, on the last occasion, not only introduced septennial in place of triennial elections, but by the same act, continued themselves in place four years beyond the term for which they were elected by the people. An attention to these dangerous practices has produced a very natural alarm in the votaries of free government, of which frequency of elections is the corner-stone; and has led them to seek for some security to liberty, against the danger to which it is exposed. Where no Constitution, paramount to the government, either existed or could be obtained, no constitutional security, similar to that established in the

authority change the constitution. Even in Great Britain, where the principles of government and the rights of citizens have been most discussed, and where we hear most about constitutional rights, the authority of Parliament is thought to be supreme and their decisions final, both in regard to passing laws as well as in changing their constitution.

[5]The Parliament has, on several occasions, changed the most important aspects of their government. For example, they have altered the time between elections and therefore their own terms of office. Recently they increased the time between elections from three to seven years, and extended their own terms four years beyond the time for which the people elected them. Taking notice of these events, those who fervently believe in democratic government, and therefore of frequent elections, have become alarmed. They have sought to protect liberty against the danger to

ORIGINAL of FEDERALIST # 53

United States, was to be attempted. Some other security, therefore, was to be sought for; and what better security would the case admit, than that of selecting and appealing to some simple and familiar portion of time, as a standard for measuring the danger of innovations, for fixing the national sentiment, and for uniting the patriotic exertions?

(6)The most simple and familiar portion of time, applicable to the subject was that of a year; and hence the doctrine has been inculcated by a laudable zeal, to erect some barrier against the gradual innovations of an unlimited government, that the advance towards tyranny was to be calculated by the distance of departure from the fixed point of annual elections. But what necessity can there be of applying this expedient to a government limited, as the federal government will be, by the authority of a paramount Constitution? Or who will pretend that the liberties of the people of America will

which it is exposed. In nations or States where the constitution was not superior to the legislature, or could not be made superior, to the legislature, liberty could not be secured by constitutional law the way that it will be in the federal government of the United States. Some other security, therefore, had to be sought.

(6)What better device could be found than selecting and trusting to the simple and familiar period of a year? This regular interval between elections became a standard by which to judge changes that might be harmful. It became a means of determining what public opinion was at regular intervals. And it provided a periodic opportunity to reunite citizens through the patriotic displays that accompany elections. The most simple and familiar portion of time to select was the year. This is where the idea came from that the erosion of a free government into a tryannical one could be

ORIGINAL of FEDERALIST # 53

not be more secure under biennial elections, unalterably fixed by such a Constitution, than those of any other nation would be, where elections were annual, or even more frequent, but subject to alterations by the ordinary power of the government?

(7)The propriety of answering this question in the affirmative will appear from several very obvious considerations.

measured by how much less than a year apart elections were to be held. People came to believe in this because of their admirable desire to protect democracy. But why should it be necessary to turn to the restraint of yearly elections when the government is already limited by the higher power of a constitution, just as the federal government will be? Who will pretend that the rights of U.S. citizens will not be more secure with elections held every two years guaranteed by the Constitution than rights in countries with annual elections that can, however, be changed by the simple passage of a law?

[7]The second question is whether it will be necessary or useful to have elections every two years for the House of Representatives. We will see from considering several very obvious points that the answer to this question is yes.

ORIGINAL of FEDERALIST # 53

(8)No man can be a competent legislator who does not add to an upright intention and a sound judgment a certain degree of knowledge of the subjects on which he is to legislate. A part of this knowledge may be acquired by means of information which lie within the compass of men in private as well as public stations. Another part can only be attained, or at least thoroughly attained, by actual experience in the station which requires the use of it. The period of service, ought, therefore, in all such cases, to bear some proportion to the extent of practical knowledge requisite to the due performance of the service.

(9)The period of legislative service established in most of the States for the more numerous branch is, as we have seen, one year. The question then may be put into this simple form: does the period of two years bear no greater proportion to the knowledge requisite for federal legislation than one year does to the State legislation?

MODERN version of FEDERALIST # 53

[8]No man can be a competent law-maker who does not possess, in addition to good intentions and sound judgment, some knowledge of the subjects about which he is supposed to make laws. Part of this may be the common knowledge that is available to anyone in business or government. Another part, however, can only be acquired on the job. The length of a term of elected office should, therefore, be related to the amount of practical knowledge necessary to do the job.

[9]In most States, the term of office for representatives to their assemblies (the State equivalent of the House of Representatives) is, as we have seen, one year. The question may be put into this simple form: isn't the period of two years for a federal legislator in the same proportion to the amount of knowledge required for the job, as a one-year term is, at the State level, to the amount of knowledge required for that job?

ORIGINAL of FEDERALIST # 53

The very statement of the question, in this form, suggests the answer that ought to be given to it.

(10)In a single State, the requisite knowledge relates to the existing laws which are uniform throughout the State, and with which all the citizens are more or less conversant; and to the general affairs of the State, which lie within a small compass, are not very diversified, and occupy much of the attention and conversation of every class of people.

(11)The great theatre of the United States presents a very different scene. The laws are so far from being uniform, that they vary in every State; whilst the public affairs of the Union are spread throughout a very extensive region, and are extremely diversified by the local affairs connected with them, and can with difficulty be correctly learnt in any other place than in the central councils' to which a knowledge of them will be brought

MODERN version of FEDERALIST # 53

When the question is put like this, the answer is obvious.

(10)The knowledge required of State legislators relates to laws that are the same throughout that one State and with which most citizens are familiar. They must also know about the general affairs of the State. These are on a small scale, they are not highly diversified, and they are common knowledge to most people within the State.

(11)The size of the United States presents a different case. State laws differ from State to State, while the national business of the country comes from a large territory and the great diversity of many regions of the country. A knowledge of the needs of the nation can be most easily learned in the national legislature, the U.S. Congress. Members of Congress will bring that knowledge to Congress from every part of the wide country.

ORIGINAL of FEDERALIST # 53

by the representatives of every part of the empire. Yet some knowledge of the affairs, and even of the laws, of all the States, ought to be possessed by the members from each of the States.

[12]How can foreign trade be properly regulated by uniform laws, without some acquaintance with the commerce, the ports, the usages, and the regulations of the different States? How can the trade between the different States be duly regulated, without some knowledge of their relative situations in these and other respects? How can taxes be judiciously imposed and effectually collected, if they be not accommodated to the different laws and local circumstances relating to these objects in the different States? How can uniform regulations for the militia be duly provided, without a similar knowledge of many internal circumstances by which the States are distinguished from each other? These are the principal objects of federal legislation,

Some knowledge of the affairs, and even of the laws, of the States, ought to be possessed by Congress members from each of the States.

[12]How can they properly regulate foreign trade by uniform laws, without some knowledge of the commerce, the ports, the regular operations and regulations of the different States? How can trade between the different States be fairly regulated without some knowledge of how internal conditions differ from State to State? How can taxes be fairly imposed and efficiently collected, if they do not account for the differences between states? How can standard regulations for the militia be established without a knowledge of the internal conditions of States? These are the main subjects of federal laws and they strongly suggest the wide scope of knowledge that a federal legislator must acquire. There are also other less important

ORIGINAL of FEDERALIST # 53

and suggest most forcibly the extensive information which the representatives ought to acquire. The other interior objects will require a proportional degree of information with regard to them.

[13]It is true that all these difficulties will, by degrees, be very much diminished. The most laborious task will be the proper inauguration of the government and the primeval formation of a federal code. Improvements on the first draughts will every year become both easier and fewer. Past transactions of the government will be a ready and accurate source of information to new members. The affairs of the Union will become more and more objects of curiosity and conversation among the citizens at large. And the increased intercourse among those of different States will contribute not a little to diffuse a mutual knowledge of their affairs, as this again will contribute to a general assimilation of their manners and laws. But with

subjects which require proportionately less knowledge.

[13] After the new Constitution takes effect, the hardest work will certainly be done first and then things will get easier as time goes by. The greatest labor will be the proper beginning and opening of the new government, and the writing of the basic federal laws. Improvements on these first attempts will be easier and fewer as the years go by. Past actions of the government will become available as an accurate source of information to new members of Congress. The affairs of the nation will increasingly capture the interest of the public and become the subject of their conversations. As citizens of different States interact with one another, their knowledge about what is going on in the other States will increase considerably. They will gradually learn to accept the laws and manners of each other. But even with all of these

ORIGINAL of FEDERALIST # 53

all these abatements, the business of federal legislation must continue so far to exceed, both in novelty and difficulty, the legislative business of a single State, as to justify the longer period of service assigned to those who are to transact it.

(14)A branch of knowledge which belongs to the acquirements of a federal representative, and which has not been mentioned is that of foreign affairs. In regulating our own commerce he ought to be not only acquainted with the treaties between the United States and other nations, but also with the commercial policy and laws of other nations. He ought not to be altogether ignorant of the law of nations; for that, as far as it is a proper object of municipal legislation, is submitted to the federal government. And although the House of Representatives is not immediately to participate in foreign negotiations and arrangements, yet from the

MODERN version of FEDERALIST # 53

moderating influences, the business of a federal legislator will always be greater in both novelty and difficulty than the business of a State legislator. Therefore a longer term of office for the federal legislator will continue to be justified.

[14]I have not yet mentioned one branch of knowledge that a federal legislator must be familiar with, which is foreign affairs. In regulating trade with other nations, he needs to be aware not just of U.S. treaties but also of the commercial policies and laws of other nations. He ought to be familiar with international law because, where international law can be affected by U.S. laws, the responsibility to reconcile the U.S. and international law will belong to the federal government. The House of Representatives does not have a direct role to play in negotiating foreign treaties and agreements. However, the Senate or other branches of government will frequently require the House to be

ORIGINAL of FEDERALIST # 53

necessary connection between the several branches of public affairs, those particular branches will frequently deserve attention in the ordinary course of legislation, and will sometimes demand particular legislative sanction and co-operation. Some portion of this knowledge may, no doubt, be acquired in a man's closet; but some of it also can only be derived from the public sources of information; and all of it will be acquired to best effect by a practical attention to the subject during the period of actual service in the legislature.

[15]There are other considerations, of less importance, perhaps, but which are not unworthy of notice. The distance which many of the representatives will be obliged to travel, and the arrangements rendered necessary by that circumstance, might be much more serious objections with fit men to this service, if limited to a single year, than if extended to two years. No argument can be drawn on this subject, from the case of

MODERN version of FEDERALIST # 53

involved in the ordinary business of law-making and will sometimes need its cooperation and approval. Part of the knowledge of international law may, no doubt, be acquired through private study, but some of it can only be gotten through governmental sources of information. Additionally, all of it is best acquired by studying the subject and putting it into practice while serving as a legislator.

[15]There are other minor points to be made in favor of a two-year term that should be mentioned. If we wish to elect the most qualified men, the distance that many of the representatives must travel and the travel arrangements that need to be made are a more serious consideration with a one-year term than a two-year term. The experience of the current legislature (the Continental Congress under the Articles of Confederation) cannot serve as a guide to us. Even though these representatives are elected for one-year terms, the State assemblies

the delegates to the existing Congress. They are elected annually, it is true; but their re-election is considered by the legislative assemblies almost as a matter of course. The election of the representatives by the people would not be governed by the same principle.

(16)A few of the members, as happens in all such assemblies, will possess superior talents; will, by frequent reelections, become members of long standing; will be thoroughly masters of the public business, and perhaps not unwilling to avail themselves of those advantages. The greater the proportion of new members, and the less the information of the bulk of the members, the more apt will they be to fall into the snares that may be laid for them. This remark is no less applicable to the relation which will subsist between the House of Representatives and the Senate.

(17)It is an inconvenience mingled with the advantages of our frequent elections even in single States,

almost always re-elect them. The election of members to the House of Representatives would operate according to a different principle because they would be elected directly by the people.

[16]As in all similar assemblies, a few members of Congress will possess superior talents. Through frequent re-election they will become long-standing members who will be master legislators, perhaps, willing to share their knowledge with other legislators. The greater the proportion of new members in the House, and the less their collective knowledge, the more likely they will be to fall into the traps that will be set for them. This is especially important when one considers the much longer terms of Senators and the Representatives' necessary connection to that part of the government.

[17]It is one of the disadvantages of frequent elections, along with their many advantages, that

ORIGINAL of FEDERALIST # 53

where they are large, and hold but one legislative session in a year, that spurious elections cannot be investigated and annulled in time for the decision to have its due effect. If a return can be obtained, no matter by what unlawful means, the irregular member, who takes his seat of course, is sure of holding it a sufficient time to answer his purposes.

[18]Hence, a very pernicious encouragement is given to the use of unlawful means, for obtaining irregular returns. Were elections for the federal legislature to be annual, this practice might become a very serious abuse, particularly in the more distant States. Each house is, as it necessarily must be, the judge of the elections, qualifications, and returns of its members; and whatever improvements may be suggested by experience, for simplifying and accelerating the process in disputed cases, so great a portion of a year would unavoidably elapse, before an illegitimate member could be dispossessed of his

questionable elections cannot be investigated and invalidated quickly enough for the decision to have a practical effect. This is true even in large States that hold elections no more frequently than once a year. After a candidate wins an election by dishonest means, assuming that he takes his seat in the legislature, he is sure to have a enough time to complete his wicked schemes.

[18]This provides a dangerous incentive to use unlawful means to win elections. If elections to the federal legislature were held annually, this practice might become a very serious abuse especially in the more distant States. The House of Representatives and the Senate are each, necessarily, the judge of the elections, qualifications and reports on elections of their respective members. Whatever improvements might be made to simplify or accelerate the investigation of questionable elections, it would still take many months to get rid of a member.

ORIGINAL of FEDERALIST # 53

seat, that the prospect of such an event would be little check to unfair and illicit means of obtaining a seat.

[19]All these considerations taken together warrant us in affirming, that biennial elections will be as useful to the affairs of the public as we have seen that they will be safe to the liberty of the people.

PUBLIUS

Therefore the prospect of eventually being unseated would probably not stop others who would try to win election by unfair and unlawful means.

[19]All of the points made in this essay taken together show that we are correct in assuming that elections held every two years for the House of Representatives will be both beneficial for the functioning of government and a safeguard for the liberty of the people.

Friend of PUBLIUS

RESEARCH AND DISCUSSION
QUESTIONS for *Federalist # 53*

1. What were the weaknesses of the government under the Articles of Confederation? Do you think that shorter terms of office made the government stronger or weaker? More or less representative?

2. In spite of the fact that most of the members of the Continental Congress were re-elected over and over again, Madison doesn't believe that will happen when the new Constitution is adopted. Was he correct? How has the incumbency rate changed since 1789?

3. How does a high incumbency rate affect the quality of our government?

4. How have term-limits affected the quality of government in the States that have adopted these limits? Has the rate of voter turnout been changed as a result? Has the power of lobbyists, special interests changed? Has the cost of elections increased or decreased as a result?

5. Madison wrote #53 to calm fears of many who believed that the federal government would have too much power. Who was correct, Madison or those who feared a strong central government? Cite historical evidence

regarding civil rights, civil liberties and property rights to support your position.

6. Write a letter to your member of Congress or your state legislature, asking for his/her opinions on national or state term limits. Would term limits make Congress more efficient, more representative, or more accountable?

7. How does the current form of the Senate differ from its original concept? Why was it changed? Did these changes have the desired results?

Author's Introduction to

THE FEDERALIST #70

The Executive Department Further
Considered
March 18, 1788

. . . .

.

By March of 1788, James Madison had returned to
Virginia to run as a delegate to the Virginia Constitutional
ratifying convention. In Madison's absence, it was left to
Alexander Hamilton alone to defend the new
Constitution. In the *Federalist #70*, Hamilton specifically
addresses concerns about the executive branch. That is,
the branch of the national government that is headed by
the President. By 1787, the time that the new
Constitution was written, a majority of citizens favored a
strong President, but that had not always been the case.

It was not the case in 1776 when Thomas Jefferson and
John Adams created the first government of the U.S.
under the Articles of Confederation. Under the Articles,
the national government had no President, no separate
executive branch, nor any chief executive.

During the colonial period under English rule, the

American colonists had resented the power and arrogance of the colonies' chief executives, the Royal Governors. Accountable only to the King, the Royal Governors had often used their powers – a veto that could not be overridden and their ability to suspend or dissolve the elected colonial assemblies – to rule as virtual dictators. As a reaction to the over-reaching power of those Governors, under the first U.S. constitution–the Articles of Confederation, all national powers were vested in the Continental Congress. There was no executive to carry out the laws, but then there were few national laws to enforce or execute. The Continental Congress primarily issued requests and requisitions that the States then enforced (or ignored) according to their own inclinations.

All of the new State constitutions, written and enacted during and after the Revolutionary War, included a chief executive in the form of a governor but required him to share power with a council. Only two States did not adopt this model. The Governors had at most a limited veto and powers that were carefully separated from those of the legislative branch (the State assemblies). The example of the States during the years under the Articles of Confederation (1781-1787) revealed the problems inherent in democratic governments. That lesson was that the legislative branch was capable of overpowering all other parts of the government. This lesson taught the next generation of leaders that an overbearing majority in the legislative branch had to be restrained.

In *The Federalist* #70, Hamilton defends the notion of an energetic, strong executive as opposed to a weaker, two or even three-person executive, or a single executive sharing power with an executive council. Even though he admits that investing all power in the hands of a single person violates the republican rule that "power is safer in the hands of a number of men than of a single man," he asserts that the President's ability to act decisively and the ability of the people to hold him accountable can only be achieved with a single President. This argument was strengthened by the almost certain knowledge that George Washington, a man who the public trusted implicitly, would be that chief executive.

Not many years were to lapse, however, before the first Secretary of the Treasury-the same Alexander Hamilton who is the author of this *"Paper"*-would recognize and use the great inherent powers of the Executive Branch to create a strong, national economic system. The subsequent history of the United States can be seen as a gradual shift of power in favor of the President, and the expansive Executive Branch of which he is the Chief Executive Officer. At times the United States has had "caretaker" Presidents who have seen themselves as custodians of the government, maintaining rather than changing or expanding the role of the President.

More often, each President has shaped the office to suit his "mandate from the people who elected him" in order to make important changes. To accomplish these goals, Presidents have energetically pursued the power needed to transform the country and thereby expanded the role of the President. These are the Presidents we remember.

On many occasions, Congress or the Supreme Court has attempted in vain to curtail the power of the President. Lately some States have defied what they see as overreaching executive power.

Modern Presidents set the agenda of Congress, especially when they are both in the same political party. Presidents are the single, recognizable leader of government. In foreign affairs, they are the Commander in Chief of the military, leading the country into war and establishing and maintaining peace. On the other hand, the power of the President domestically is constitutionally limited and primarily consists of his power to persuade others in government to enact his agenda.

The checks and balances built into the Constitution were meant to stop the President from usurping the powers of the other branches, and to prevent him from using the executive branch as a political weapon to win and maintain control over the government. The process of selecting Presidents was meant to ensure that only honorable men with great intellect and love of country would be chosen. They fervently hoped that the government they created would obviate the need for political parties and would balance one set of special interests against another, so that the interests of the people and the country, indeed of democracy itself, would be protected from what they saw as the "violence of factions."

They did not foresee the rise of highly polarized political parties, which would at times put partisan interests above the good of the nation, refusing to hold Presidents of their own party accountable for their actions. They knew that democracy could devolve into mobocracy (rule by the mob) and they built safeguards against it into the Constitution. However, they did not foresee the President as a potential instigator of that mob. They could not have known that the power of televised and on-line media in an age of extremism could intentionally deliver misinformation to the public, enabling Presidents to lead the country into harm's way instead of protecting the nation from it.

Hamilton did not foresee these developments. He argues in this *Federalist Paper* that the constraints on the President created by the new Constitution of 1787 would be enough to contain what would, of necessity, be considerable power in the hands of one man.

Terms to know before you read the essay: (see Glossary)

- republican government
- Executive branch
- Legislative branch
- Philadelphia Convention
- Unity
- Factions
- Co-presidents
- Accountability

GUIDED READING QUESTIONS for
Students to answer as you read

1. What benefits does a strong presidency provide to a representative democracy (a republic)?

2. Why does a weak executive create a bad government?

3. What according to Madison is the most necessary quality of a President?

4. In your opinion, is Madison correct when he says that decisiveness, energy, secrecy and speed are more characteristic of a person working alone than of a group of people working together? Explain the reasons for your answer. Give an example.

5. What problems might arise if the presidency was split between two people?

6. How do human weaknesses complicate decision-making according to Madison? Do you think he is correct?

7. Why is disagreement within the legislative branch beneficial while it is detrimental in the executive?

8. In what ways is accountability diminished in a system in which executive power is shared?

9. Why is a single executive safer?

"First in war, first in peace, and first in the hearts of his countrymen." George Washington was respected and trusted by the public and widely expected to be the first President under the new Constitution of 1787. He took office in 1789 and served two terms. This is the short list of Washington's accomplishments.

ORIGINAL *of Federalist #70*

[1]THERE is an idea, which is not without its advocates, that a vigorous Executive is inconsistent with the genius of republican government. The enlightened well-wishers to this species of government must at least hope that the supposition is destitute of foundation; since they can never admit its truth, without at the same time admitting the condemnation of their own principles.

[2]Energy in the Executive is a leading character in the definition of good government. It is essential to the protection of the community against foreign attacks; it is not less essential to the steady administration of the laws; to the protection of property against those irregular and high-handed combinations which sometimes interrupt the ordinary course of justice; to the security of liberty against the enterprises and assaults of ambition, of faction, and of anarchy. Every man the least conversant in Roman history, knows how often that that republic was obliged to take refuge in the absolute power of a single man,

MODERN version of Federalist #70

[1]Some people believe that a powerful presidency contradicts the most important ideals of a republican government. Those who understand and believe in democracy must hope that this belief is wrong since to agree with it would mean to condemn their own beliefs.

[2]A strong and active presidency is one of the defining characteristics of good government. It is essential to the protection of the country against foreign attacks. It is important in ensuring that the laws are consistently enforced. It is required to protect property against improper and arrogant plots against the decisions of the courts. A vigorous presidency is also important in protecting freedom from the conspiracies and attacks of those who would seize power. Anyone who is familiar with Roman history knows how often that republic found it necessary to seek protection in the absolute power of a single man, who they called by the

ORIGINAL of FEDERALIST # 70

under the formidable title of Dictator, as well against the intrigues of ambitious individuals who aspired to the tyranny, and the seditions of whole classes of the community whose conduct threatened the existence of all government, as against the invasions of external enemies who menaced the conquest and destruction of Rome.

(3)There can be no need, however, to multiply arguments or examples on this head. A feeble Executive implies a feeble execution of the government. A feeble execution is but another phrase for a bad execution; and a government ill executed, whatever it may be in theory, must be, in practice, a bad government.

(4)Taking it for granted, therefore, that all men of sense will agree in the necessity of an energetic Executive, it will only remain to inquire, what are the

fearful name of a dictator. This security was necessary to guard them from internal enemies, ambitious individuals who sought power, and whole groups of people whose treachery threatened the very existence of government. A strong executive was equally necessary to protect them against the invasion of external enemies who would have conquered and destroyed Rome.

(3)There is no need, however, for a long list of examples. A feeble presidency implies a government of weak actions and enforcement. Weak enforcement is but another name for bad enforcement. A government of weak actions, whatever it may be in theory, must be a bad government in practice.

(4)Assuming, then, that all sensible men will agree that an energetic (that is, a strong, active) presidency is necessary, we only need ask what

ORIGINAL of FEDERALIST # 70

ingredients which constitute this energy? How far can they be combined with those other ingredients which constitute safety in the republican sense? And how far does this combination characterize the plan which has been reported by the convention?

(5)*The ingredients which constitute energy in the Executive are, first, unity; secondly, duration; thirdly, an adequate provision for its support; fourthly, competent powers.*

(6)*The ingredients which constitute safety in the republican sense are, first, a due dependence on the people, secondly, a due responsibility.*

ingredients make up this energy? Whether the elements of energy can be combined with the elements that protect freedom within a republican government? And, whether the government proposed by the Philadelphia convention provides a strong presidency while safeguarding freedom.

(5)There are four ingredients that combine to create a strong presidency. The first is unity, that is, the presidency should be held by one person. The second is duration, that is, the presidency should have a relatively long term of office that is infinitely repeatable. The third is an adequate salary that cannot be increased nor decreased during a President's term in office. The fourth is sufficient power to perform the duties of the office and to provide a check on the other branches.

(6)The ingredients, which ensure that the rights of the people are safe in a republican government,

ORIGINAL of FEDERALIST # 70

(7)*Those politicians and statesmen, who have been the most celebrated for the soundness of their principles and for the justice of their views, have declared in favor of a single Executive and a numerous legislature. They have with great propriety, considered energy as the most necessary qualification of the former, and have regarded this as most applicable to power in a single hand, while they have, with equal propriety, considered the latter as best adapted to deliberation and wisdom, and best calculated to conciliate the confidence of the people and to secure their privileges and interests.*

(8)*That unity is conducive to energy will not be disputed. Decision, activity, secrecy, and despatch will generally characterize the proceedings of one man in a much more eminent degree than the proceedings of any*

are a proper dependence on the will of the people, and accountability.

[7]Those politicians and statesmen who have been known for their wisdom and sense of justice have favored a one-man presidency and a large legislature. They have appropriately regarded the ability to act as the most necessary quality of a president and considered the single presidency most likely to embody that quality. While they also have believed that the ability to debate and discuss, and to exercise wisdom are the characteristics of the legislative branch. This ability enables the legislature to win the confidence of the people, to pursue their interests and to secure their rights.

[8]The claim that unity (a single presidency) is more likely to result in an energetic presidency will not be disputed. Decisiveness, energy, secrecy and speed are qualities that will far more often characterize the actions of one man than of many

ORIGINAL of FEDERALIST #70

greater number; and in proportion as the number is increased, these qualities will be diminished.

(9)This unity may be destroyed in two ways: either by vesting the power in two or more magistrates of equal dignity and authority; or by vesting it ostensibly in one man, subject, in whole or in part, to the control and co-operation of others, in the capacity of counsellors to him. Of the first, the two Consuls of Rome may serve as an example; of the last, we shall find examples in the constitutions of several of the States. New York and New Jersey, if I recollect right, are the only States which have intrusted the executive authority wholly to single men.[1] Both these methods of destroying the unity of the Executive have their

---

[1.] New York has no council except for the single purpose of appointing to offices in New Jersey has a council whom the governor may consult. But I think, from the terms of the constitution, their resolutions do not bind him.

MODERN version of FEDERALIST # 70

men working together. In fact, these qualities will decrease as the number of people working together increases.

[9]Unity may be destroyed in two ways: either by giving authority to two or more officials with equal power and status, or by giving formal authority to one man but making him dependent on the advice and cooperation of a council. The dual consuls (chief executives) of the Romans provide us with an example of the first method of destroying unity. In the constitutions of several of the States, we see examples of the second method, that is, requiring the executive to share power with a council. New York and New Jersey, if I remember correctly, are the only states whose governors are trusted with the sole power of the executive.[1] Both

---

[1] In New York, a council exists only for the purpose of appointing officials. New Jersey has a council, which the governor may consult for advice, but he is not obligated to follow their advice.

ORIGINAL of FEDERALIST #70

partisans; but the votaries of an executive council are the most numerous.   They are both liable, if not to equal, to similar objections, and may in most lights be examined in conjunction.

(10)*The experience of other nations will afford little instruction on this head.   As far, however, as it teaches any thing, it teaches us not to be enamoured of plurality in the Executive.   We have seen that the Achaeans, on an experiment of two Praetors, were induced to abolish one.   The Roman history records many instances of mischiefs to the republic from the dissensions between the Consuls, and between the military Tribunes, who were at times substituted for the Consuls.   But it gives us no specimens of any peculiar advantages derived to the state from the circumstance of the plurality of those magistrates.   That the dissensions between them were not more frequent or more fatal, is a matter of astonishment, until we advert to the position in which the*

methods of destroying the unity of the presidency have their supporters, but most of these people would destroy it by making the president dependent upon a council. Similar objections can be made to both methods and so, to some extent, they can be discussed at the same time.

[10]Even though there is little that the experiences of other nations can teach us, we should learn from them not to be enthusiastic about a plural executive. We have seen that the Achaeans (one of the four tribes of ancient Greece) found it necessary to abolish the office of one of their two Praetors (chief administrators). Roman history records many examples of the damage to that republic caused by disagreements between their consuls, or between their military tribunes who were sometimes substituted for the consuls. However, that same history yields no examples of the advantages of a plural presidency. We may find

republic was almost continually placed, and to the prudent policy pointed out by the circumstances of the state, and pursued by the Consuls, of making a division of the government between them. The patricians engaged in a perpetual struggle with the plebeians for the preservation of their ancient authorities and dignities; the Consuls, who were generally chosen out of the former body, were commonly united by the personal interest they had in the defense of the privileges of their order.

(11)In addition to this motive of union, after the arms of the republic had considerably expanded the bounds of its empire, it became an established custom with the Consuls to divide the administration between themselves by lot one of them remaining at Rome to govern the city and its environs, the other taking the command in the more distant provinces. This expedient

it astonishing that the disagreements of the consuls were not more frequent or more fatal, until we consider that the consuls almost always adopted the wise policy of dividing the government between the themselves. The specific circumstances of the Roman republic created the necessity and the occasion for cooperation between the consuls. The patricians (the Roman aristocracy) were in an almost constant struggle against the plebeians (commoners) to preserve their traditional status and powers. The two consuls were generally patricians and so they were united by a common personal interest in defending the privileges of their class.

[11]Also, after military conquests had greatly enlarged the empire, it was the custom for the two consuls to divide their duties between them by a lottery. One consul governed Rome and the adjacent areas, while the other ruled over the provinces. This solution undoubtedly prevented

must, no doubt, have had great influence in preventing those collisions and rivalships which might otherwise have embroiled the peace of the republic.

(12)But quitting the dim light of historical research, attaching ourselves purely to the dictates of reason and good sense, we shall discover much greater cause to reject than to approve the idea of plurality in the Executive, under any modification whatever.

(13)Wherever two or more persons are engaged in any common enterprise or pursuit, there is always danger of difference of opinion. If it be a public trust or office, in which they are clothed with equal dignity and authority, there is peculiar danger of personal emulation and even animosity. From either, and especially from all these causes, the most bitter dissensions are apt to spring. Whenever these happen, they lessen the respectability, weaken the authority, and distract the plans and operation of those whom they divide. If they should

rivalry and conflict that otherwise might have caused turmoil within the republic.

[12]But leaving the dim light of historical research and relying instead on logic and common sense exclusively, we will find many more reasons to reject the idea of a plural presidency than to accept it, regardless of how it is organized.

[13]Whenever two or more people are engaged in any common business or pursuit, there is always the danger of a difference of opinion. If they hold public offices, which confer equal powers and status, there is a special danger of personal rivalry and even animosity. From either, or all of these causes, the most bitter disputes are apt to spring. And whenever disputes arise, they lessen the respectability of, weaken the authority of, and distract from their duties, those whom they divide. If these disputes should occur between the officers

ORIGINAL of FEDERALIST # 70

unfortunately assail the supreme executive magistracy of a country, consisting of a plurality of persons, they might impede or frustrate the most important measures of the government, in the most critical emergencies of the state. And what is still worse, they might split the community into the most violent and irreconcilable factions, adhering differently to the different individuals who composed the magistracy.

(13)Men often oppose a thing, merely because they have had no agency in planning it, or because it may have been planned by those whom they dislike. But if they have been consulted, and have happened to disapprove, opposition then becomes, in their estimation, an indispensable duty of self-love. They seem to think themselves bound in honor, and by all the motives of personal infallibility, to defeat the success of what has been resolved upon contrary to their sentiments. Men of upright, benevolent tempers have too many opportunities

of a plural presidency, the highest executive office, they might interfere with the most important policies of the government during the most critical emergencies of a nation. Or worse still, they might split the country into violent and irreconcilable factions each loyal to one of the co-presidents.

[13]Men often oppose a thing merely because they have had no part in planning it, or because it was the idea of someone they dislike. And, if they were consulted and disapproved of the plan, then their ego is threatened and their opposition becomes a matter of pride. They are convinced that they are right and think that they are honor-bound to prevent the success of a plan that was decided against their wishes. Moral and good-natured men have too often witnessed with horror the desperate acts committed because of this kind of ill-will. How often are the important interests of society sacrificed to vanity, conceit and stubbornness?

ORIGINAL of FEDERALIST # 70

of remarking, with horror, to what desperate lengths this disposition is sometimes carried, and how often the great interests of society are sacrificed to the vanity, to the conceit, and to the obstinacy of individuals, who have credit enough to make their passions and their caprices interesting to mankind. Perhaps the question now before the public may, in its consequences, afford melancholy proofs of the effects of this despicable frailty, or rather detestable vice, in the human character.

[14]Upon the principles of a free government, inconveniences from the source just mentioned must necessarily be submitted to in the formation of the legislature; but it is unnecessary, and therefore unwise, to introduce them into the constitution of the Executive

[15] . It is here too that they may be most pernicious. In the legislature, promptitude of decision is oftener an evil than a benefit. The differences of opinion, and the jarrings of parties in that department of the

Often the individuals involved are well trusted so that their disputes spread to the public. Unfortunately, as we debate the ratification of the Constitution, it may be sadly proven to the public through its consequences, that this terrible weakness, or rather hateful vice, is part of human nature.

[14]In regard to democratic government, the problems of egotism and stubbornness are necessary evils in a legislative body, but it is unneccssary and therefore unwise to build them into the structure of the executive branch.

[15]It is here, too, that they may cause the greatest harm.In the legislature, quick decision-making is more often an evil than a benefit. The differences in opinion, the clashing of parties in that branch of the government, though it may sometimes interfere with beneficial plans, also often promotes debate

ORIGINAL of FEDERALIST # 70

government though they may sometimes obstruct salutary plans, yet often promote deliberation and circumspection, and serve to check excesses in the majority.

(16)When a resolution too is once taken, the opposition must be at an end. That resolution is a law, and resistance to it punishable. But no favorable circumstances palliate or atone for the disadvantages of dissension in the executive department. Here, they are pure and unmixed. There is no point at which they cease to operate.

(17)They serve to embarrass and weaken the execution of the plan or measure to which they relate, from the first step to the final conclusion of it. They constantly counteract those qualities in the Executive which are the most necessary ingredients in its composition, vigor and expedition, and this without any counter-balancing good. In the conduct of war, in which

and careful consideration, and may serve as a check on the strong feelings of a majority.

[16]When the legislature makes a final decision, opposition to it must end. It becomes law and breaking the law is punishable. But in the executive branch there are no advantages to disagreement that would weigh against its disadvantages. Nor are there procedures that would modify its effects. In the executive, the disadvantages of internal conflict are not balanced by advantages. Neither is there a point where they must stop.

[17]They would complicate and weaken the execution of any plan or policy from its first step to its final conclusion. The effects of conflict within the executive would constantly counteract those qualities that are the most necessary ingredients of the presidency--strength and swiftness--without any counterbalancing good. During a war when the energy of the executive provides the main defense

the energy of the Executive is the bulwark of the national security, every thing would be to be apprehended from its plurality.

[18]*It must be confessed that these observations apply with principal weight to the first case supposed that is, to a plurality of magistrates of equal dignity and authority a scheme, the advocates for which are not likely to form a numerous sect; but they apply, though not with equal, yet with considerable weight to the project of a council, whose concurrence is made constitutionally necessary to the operations of the ostensible Executive. An artful cabal in that council would be able to distract and to enervate the whole system of administration. If no such cabal should exist, the mere diversity of views and opinions would alone be sufficient to tincture the exercise of the executive authority with a spirit of habitual feebleness and dilatoriness.*

of the nation's security, we would have much to fear from a plural presidency.

[18]It must be confessed that the objections I have so far raised apply to a plural executive whose members would have equal status and authority, and few will support this idea. However, almost all of the arguments against a plural executive can also be made against a single executive who is dependent on the cooperation of a council. A clever conspiracy within the council would be able to distract and agitate the whole executive branch. And even if no such conspiracy occurred, the mere diversity of views and opinions alone would be enough to introduce delay and weakness into executive action.

ORIGINAL of FEDERALIST # 70

[19]*But one of the weightiest objections to a plurality in the Executive, and which lies as much against the last as the first plan, is, that it tends to conceal faults and destroy responsibility. Responsibility is of two kinds, to censure and to punish. The first is the more important of the two, especially in an elective office. Man, in public trust, will much oftener act in such a manner as to render him unworthy of being any longer trusted, than in such a manner as to make him obnoxious to legal punishment. But the multiplication of the Executive adds to the difficulty of detection in either case.*

[20]*It often becomes impossible, amidst mutual accusations, to determine on whom the blame or the punishment of a pernicious measure, or series of pernicious measures, ought really to fall. It is shifted from one to another with so much dexterity, and under such plausible appearances, that the public opinion is left*

MODERN version of FEDERALIST # 70

[19]But one of the most serious objections to a plural executive--whether of several co-equals or of a chief executive with a council--is that it obscures mistakes and destroys accountability. There are two parts of accountability, blaming and punishing. The first is the more important of the two, especially as it applies to elected offices. Men in positions of public trust are more likely to act in ways that make them less trustworthy, rather than they are actually to break the law and so be liable for punishment. But a plural executive makes it more difficult to detect either kind of wrongdoing.

[20]It often becomes impossible amidst mutual accusations to know whom to blame or punish for disastrous policies. The blame is shifted with such ease and with so many believable explanations that the public is unable to decide who is the guilty party. The circumstances surrounding a misdeed or mistake are sometimes very complicated. When a

ORIGINAL of FEDERALIST # 70

in suspense about the real author. The circumstances which may have led to any national miscarriage or misfortune are sometimes so complicated that, where there are a number of actors who may have had different degrees and kinds of agency, though we may clearly see upon the whole that there has been mismanagement, yet it may be impracticable to pronounce to whose account the evil which may have been incurred is truly chargeable.

[21]"I was overruled by my council. The council were so divided in their opinions that it was impossible to obtain any better resolution on the point." These and similar pretexts are constantly at hand, whether true or false. And who is there that will either take the trouble or incur the odium, of a strict scrutiny into the secret springs of the transaction? Should there be found a citizen zealous enough to undertake the unpromising task, if there happen to be collusion between the parties

number of people had different degrees and kinds of involvement in it, we may clearly see that there has been wrong-doing but not be able to accurately fix blame on anyone.

[21]"I was overruled by my council. The council were so divided in their opinions that it was impossible to reach an agreement on this point." These and similar excuses are always available, whether they are true or false. And who will take the trouble and make themselves unpopular by looking more deeply into the matter? And even if such an enthusiastic, hardworking citizen could be found to undertake this thankless task, he might not be able to do it. If some of the individuals involved conspired together it would be very easy for them to give such ambiguous accounts of what happened that no one would be able to tell what the actual conduct of any of them had been.

ORIGINAL of FEDERALIST # 70

concerned, how easy it is to clothe the circumstances with so much ambiguity, as to render it uncertain what was the precise conduct of any of those parties?

[22]In the single instance in which the governor of this State is coupled with a council, that is, in the appointment to offices, we have seen the mischiefs of it in the view now under consideration. Scandalous appointments to important offices have been made. Some cases, indeed, have been so flagrant that ALL PARTIES have agreed in the impropriety of the thing. When inquiry has been made, the blame has been laid by the governor on the members of the council, who, on their part, have charged it upon his nomination; while the people remain altogether at a loss to determine by whose influence their interests have been committed to hands so unqualified and so manifestly improper. In tenderness to individuals, I forbear to descend to particulars.

[22]The actions of the governor of this State (New York) must depend on a council only in the matter of appointing officials, and we have seen the problems caused by a lack of accountability because of this arrangement. Scandalous appointments to important offices have been made. Some appointments, indeed, have been so outrageous that everyone involved has agreed that they were improper. When questioned about it, the governor has blamed the members of the council who in turn blame the governor. In the meantime, the people of New York don't know whether to blame the council or the governor for having entrusted their interests to someone so incompetent and clearly inappropriate. Out of concern for the feelings of others, I will not go into details about these matters.

ORIGINAL of FEDERALIST # 70

[23]*It is evident from these considerations, that the plurality of the Executive tends to deprive the people of the two greatest securities they can have for the faithful exercise of any delegated power, first, the restraints of public opinion, which lose their efficacy, as well on account of the division of the censure attendant on bad measures among a number, as on account of the uncertainty on whom it ought to fall; and, secondly, the opportunity of discovering with facility and clearness the misconduct of the persons they trust, in order either to their removal from office or to their actual punishment in cases which admit of it.*

[24]*In England, the king is a perpetual magistrate; and it is a maxim which has obtained for the sake of the public peace, that he is unaccountable for his administration, and his person sacred. Nothing, therefore, can be wiser in that kingdom, than to annex to the king a constitutional council, who may be responsible*

MODERN version of FEDERALIST # 70

[23]It is clear from this discussion that having a plural executive deprives citizens of their two greatest safeguards against the abuse of those powers that they have entrusted to elected officials. First, public criticism loses its effectiveness, both because it is spread among a number of individuals and because it is not clear which officials truly deserve to be blamed. Second, with a plural executive, citizens will have more difficulty discovering with certainty that misconduct has occurred so that those responsible may be removed from office or punished.

[24]In England, the King's term in office is unlimited. In order to maintain a peaceful society, they have accepted the rule that he is not accountable for his management of public affairs, and that his physical existence is sacred. Given this arrangement, nothing could be wiser than to attach to the monarchy a constitutional council that is

ORIGINAL of FEDERALIST # 70

to the nation for the advice they give. Without this, there would be no responsibility whatever in the executive department an idea inadmissible in a free government.

But even there the king is not bound by the resolutions of his council, though they are answerable for the advice they give. He is the absolute master of his own conduct in the exercise of his office, and may observe or disregard the counsel given to him at his sole discretion.

[25]But in a republic, where every magistrate ought to be personally responsible for his behavior in office the reason which in the British Constitution dictates the propriety of a council, not only ceases to apply, but turns against the institution. In the monarchy of Great Britain, it furnishes a substitute for the prohibited responsibility of the chief magistrate, which serves in some degree as a hostage to the national justice for his good behavior. In the American republic, it would serve to destroy, or would greatly diminish, the

MODERN version of FEDERALIST # 70

answerable to the nation for the advice they give. There would be no accountability at all in the executive branch without this council, and that would be unacceptable in free government. But even in this case, the King does not have to take the council's advice. Even though they are responsible to the people for the advice they give, he is answerable to no one for his official conduct, and the decision to accept or refuse the council's advice is his alone.

[25] But the reason for the executive council in Britain does not apply in a republic like ours where every official ought to be personally responsible for his behavior in office. In fact the principle works in reverse here. In the monarchy of Great Britain, the council provides a degree of accountability that the King must be above. They serve, in part, to guarantee the King's good behavior. In the American republic, an executive council would

ORIGINAL of FEDERALIST # 70

intended and necessary responsibility of the Chief Magistrate himself.

(26)The idea of a council to the Executive, which has so generally obtained in the State constitutions, has been derived from that maxim of republican jealousy which considers power as safer in the hands of a number of men than of a single man. If the maxim should be admitted to be applicable to the case, I should contend that the advantage on that side would not counterbalance the numerous disadvantages on the opposite side. But I do not think the rule at all applicable to the executive power. I clearly concur in opinion, in this particular, with a writer whom the celebrated Junius pronounces to be "deep, solid, and ingenious," that "the executive power is more easily confined when it is ONE"; that it is far more safe there should be a single object for the jealousy and watchfulness of the people; and, in a word, that all

destroy, or at least greatly diminish, the intended and necessary responsibility of the President.

[26]The idea of a council to the Executive has been widely accepted in the States' constitutions. It comes from that famous rule of republican caution: power is safer in the hands of a number of men than of a single man. Even if this rule applied to executive councils, I would argue that the advantages to a plural executive were far outweighed by its disadvantages. But I do not think the rule applies at all to the powers of the executive branch. On this point, I agree with a writer, whom the celebrated Junius (an British critic of the Prime Minister) proclaims to be "deep, solid, and ingenious," that "the executive power is more easily confined when it is one." It is far safer to have just one official who the people must carefully watch. Having more than one chief executive is more dangerous than helpful to liberty.

ORIGINAL of FEDERALIST # 70

multiplication of the Executive is rather dangerous than friendly to liberty.

[27]A little consideration will satisfy us, that the species of security sought for in the multiplication of the Executive, is unattainable. Numbers must be so great as to render combination difficult, or they are rather a source of danger than of security. The united credit and influence of several individuals must be more formidable to liberty, than the credit and influence of either of them separately. When power, therefore, is placed in the hands of so small a number of men, as to admit of their interests and views being easily combined in a common enterprise, by an artful leader, it becomes more liable to abuse, and more dangerous when abused, than if it be lodged in the hands of one man; who, from the very circumstance of his being alone, will be more narrowly watched and more readily suspected, and who cannot unite so great a mass of influence as when he is

MODERN version of FEDERALIST # 70

[27]If we think about this for a minute, we will see that the kind of security that we are looking for when we turn to a plural executive is unattainable. The number of executive officers must be so great that they will not easily be able to conspire together. Otherwise they will be a source of danger rather than of security. The sum of their reputations and influence must be more threatening to a free society than the reputation and influence of any of them individually. Power placed in the hands of a small group of men will allow a skillful leader to combine their interests and views in order to form a common purpose. Thus, power is more likely to be abused, and more dangerous when abused, than if it were in the hands of single man. Because he is alone, the sole executive will be more closely watched and more quickly suspected. He will be less able to amass influence than when he is united with others. In terms of the abuse of power, the

ORIGINAL of FEDERALIST # 70

associated with others. The Decemvirs of Rome, whose name denotes their number, TEN were more to be dreaded in their usurpation than any ONE of them would have been.

[28]No person would think of proposing an Executive much more numerous than that body; from six to a dozen have been suggested for the number of the council. The extreme of these numbers, is not too great for an easy combination; and from such a combination America would have more to fear, than from the ambition of any single individual. A council to a magistrate, who is himself responsible for what he does, are generally nothing better than a clog upon his good intentions, are often the instruments and accomplices of his bad and are almost always a cloak to his faults.

[29]I forbear to dwell upon the subject of expense; though it be evident that if the council should be numerous enough to answer the principal end aimed at

decemvirs (group of ten executives) of Rome were more to be feared than any one of them alone.

[28]No one would think of proposing a co-presidency of much more than the number of these ten magistrates. From six to twelve have been suggested for the number of the council. Even twelve is not too many to form a faction. America would have more to fear from such a combination than from the ambition of any single individual. If an executive officer is accountable for what he does, then a council will do little more than frustrate his good intentions, act as the instruments through which he accomplishes his bad intentions, or become his accomplices, and almost always will provide a way to hide his faults

[29]I do not wish to dwell upon the subject of expense, however it should be clear that if there were enough individuals in a plural executive to do the job, their salaries would amount to a significant

by the institution, the salaries of the members, who must be drawn from their homes to reside at the seat of government, would form an item in the catalogue of public expenditures too serious to be incurred for an object of equivocal utility.

[30]I will only add that, prior to the appearance of the Constitution, I rarely met with an intelligent man from any of the States, who did not admit, as the result of experience, that the UNITY of the executive of this State was one of the best of the distinguishing features of our constitution.

PUBLIUS

item in the budget. Their pay must be high enough to compensate them for having to leave their homes and live in the capital city. This is too much to spend for something that is probably useless.

[30]I will only add that before the new federal Constitution was written, I rarely spoke with an intelligent man from any of the States who did not admit that from his experience the UNITY of the executive in New York State was one of the best features of our State constitution.

Friend of PUBLIUS

RESEARCH AND DISCUSSION QUESTIONS for *Federalist # 70*

1. How do the powers of the U.S. President compare to those of the U.K. Prime Minister? How do the powers of the U.S. President compare to the President and Prime Ministers of semi-presidential systems such as France or Germany?

2. Why is the War Powers Act considered by many to be an unconstitutional over-reach by Congress?

3. Madison believed that the Electoral College would ensure that only the best-qualified and respected people would become President. How has the role of the Electoral College changed since 1788?

4. What changes could be made to our manner of electing a President that might produce an outcome that is more representative of the will of the voters?

5. How do the realities of modern Presidential campaigns affect the quality of the candidates that are eventually chosen?

6. What are the pros and cons of exclusively using public funding with which to finance Presidential campaigns?

7. How do Presidential candidates attempt to use the media to win election? How does the modern media effect the public's perception of Presidential candidates?

Author's Introduction to
THE FEDERALIST #78
May 28, 1788

. . . .

In this essay, Hamilton is writing in support of strong, independent federal courts (the judicial branch). He believed that the power of judicial review was an essential part of that strength. Judicial review is the power of the courts to declare that acts of the other branches of government are unconstitutional, and thus unenforceable. (nationalparalegal.edu) The only court created by the Constitution was the Supreme Court. The rest of the federal courts were created by the *Judicial Act of 1789*, which passed the first time that the new U.S. Congress met. Judicial review was not spelled out in the Constitution but most well-informed readers at the time would have assumed that the Supreme Court would have to have judicial review. It was made official in one of the Supreme Court's earliest decisions, Marbury v. Madison (1803).

Although many agreed with Hamilton that the judicial branch would be the weakest of the three branches of government, they worried that if the Supreme Court could overturn any law of any State, the sovereignty and independence of the States would be eliminated. It is, in part, these fears that Hamilton is addressing.

It was broadly agreed that a federal judiciary branch was needed, as Hamilton asserts in *Federalist #78*. If there was to be a national government with the power to enact laws, inevitably those laws would be broken and disputes would arise. In fact, conflict between various states had already occurred during the period of Confederation when there existed only a judiciary committee in the Continental Congress to resolve them. The absence of an executive power under the Articles of Confederation meant that the decisions of this committee could be ignored with impunity.

Even though there was general agreement that a national judiciary was necessary, the relative strength of that branch of the government was hotly debated. Two features of the proposed judicial branch were particularly worrying to the Antifederalists, the power of judicial review and life-tenure for judges. Although juries, which were drawn from the ranks of the citizenry, were representative and trustworthy, judges were seen as an unelected elite and were not trusted to support the will of the people. The States' constitutions had granted judges either long terms of office or the power to overturn state laws but not both of these powers simultaneously. Some states, New York for example, had committees to review constitutional challenges. It was feared that if the courts could overturn laws passed by the people's representatives, this unelected elitist institution would be placed above the will of the people.

The Antifederalist author whose pen-name was Brutus, writing in the New York Journal newspaper predicted that rather than be limited strictly by precedent and the words of the Constitution, federal judges would make decisions based on what they believed was the "spirit' of the Constitution. This is precisely the charge made today by those who believe in a strict interpretation of the Constitution guided by the original intent of its authors. Brutus further claimed that federal judges would use their decisions to increase the powers of the federal government at the expense of the states. Many people have experienced the implementation of court rulings from *Gibbons v. Ogden* (1824) to *Roe v. Wade* (1973) as a long string of violations of States' rights.

Against this background of mistrust, Hamilton argued that a strong, independent judiciary was of vital importance. He pointed out that the judicial branch lacks any power to enforce its decisions relying instead on the executive branch. Life tenure, he wrote, is a necessary defense for the courts. It is the only guarantee that the judiciary will not become a political tool of one of the other branches. The court must also be protected from the pressure of popular majorities. It must have the independence to uphold the Constitution and, if necessary, to protect the rights of unpopular groups or individuals against the wishes of the majority. In North Carolina and Rhode Island, courts had been censured and judges dismissed when they dared to rule in favor of creditors who were being forced to accept nearly worthless paper money. In New York, the highest court lost its popular support and therefore its authority when it ruled against a state law that violated a U.S. peace treaty, a mandate of Congress, and the laws of nations.

Hamilton argued in *Federalist #78* that the right of judicial review, rather than placing the courts above the elected representatives of the people, merely gave the courts the right to uphold the fundamental expression of the peoples' will – the Constitution–against temporary biases, schemes of legislators or interest groups who might occasionally gain popular support. If the people want to alter their fundamental law, the Constitution could be revised. In the meantime, the Supreme Court must have sufficient power to protect it.

As to the charge that federal judges would use the power of the courts to enlarge the sphere of federal powers, he asserts without proof that they will decide federal versus state questions with impartiality. This is one of the weakest points in his argument. Just as the Antifederalists predicted, the right of judicial review plus the Supremacy Clause which places federal law above State law together with the ambiguous phrasing of much of the Constitution have permitted federal courts to recast the balance of power in favor of the federal government.

It can be argued that this increase of federal power has been necessitated by global events, national challenges, and changes in communication and transportation that have knit us together as a nation more strongly than was the case in the 18th century. It can be argued that we benefitted as individuals and as a nation when the rights of U.S. citizenship were fully defined and uniformly enforced by the federal government. However, it is very difficult to claim that the modern balance of power between the federal and States' governments is exactly the one described by the Constitution or the one promised by proponents like Hamilton.

Terms to know before you read the essay: (see Glossary)

- Fundamental
- Judicial review
- Judiciary
- Judicial branch
- Precedents
- Moderate (adj)

GUIDED READING QUESTIONS for
Students to answer as you read

1. What governments already granted judges life tenure when this essay was written?

2. What protection do unlimited terms of office give to judges?

3. In what ways is the judicial branch the weakest branch?

4. What would happen if the judiciary could not maintain its separation from the other branches?

5. How does a strong judiciary branch help to maintain limited government and therefore individual rights?

6. Why is it true that any law that contradicts the Constitution must be invalid?

7. Why can't the legislature decide whether or not laws are constitutional?

8. If a court can over-ride laws passed by the legislature, then the judicial branch must be more powerful than the legislative branch. Yet Hamilton says that it is not. What argument does he use to prove that it isn't?

12. Why does Hamilton say that it is pointless to argue that the power of judicial review will enable judges to rule in ways that will serve only their own interests?

13. Why is life tenure necessary in order that the judicial branch can protect individual rights against the demands of a majority of the pubic?

14. Why shouldn't people be able to act in ways that violate constitutional principles if they do not agree with the Constitution?

15. How does everyone benefit when the rights of individuals or groups of individuals are protected?

17. Why would a federal judge need to be a person of great skill and learning? Why might limited terms of office discourage the best-qualified people from accepting judgeships?

TEARING DOWN STATUE OF GEORGE III.

ORIGINAL of Federalist #78

(1)WE PROCEED now to an examination of the judiciary department of the proposed government.

(2)In unfolding the defects of the existing Confederation, the utility and necessity of a federal judicature have been clearly pointed out. It is none the less necessary to recapitulate the considerations there urged, as the propriety of the institution in the abstract is not disputed; the only questions which have been raised being relative to the manner of constituting it, and to its extent. To these points, therefore, our observations shall be confined.

(3)The manner of constituting it seems to embrace these several objects: 1st. The mode of appointing the judges. 2d. The tenure by which they are to hold their

MODERN version of Federalist #78

[1]NOW we turn our attention to an examination of the judiciary branch of the government proposed by the Constitution.

[2]The usefulness and necessity of a federal court system have been clearly pointed out in previous _Federalist Papers_ as part of the discussion of the shortcomings of the government under the Articles of Confederation.* It is not necessary to restate those arguments here because the importance of having some sort of federal judiciary is not being disputed. The only questions that have not been answered concern the manner in which the judicial branch is to be constructed and the extent of its powers. In this essay therefore, we will limit our discussion to those questions.

[3]The question of how the judicial branch is to be constructed includes several parts: First. The

---

* Under the Articles of Confederation, there was no national court system, only the courts of the various States.

ORIGINAL of FEDERALIST # 78

places. 3d. The partition of the judiciary authority between different courts, and their relations to each other.

(4)First. As to the mode of appointing the judges; this is the same with that of appointing the

officers of the Union in general, and has been so fully discussed in the two last numbers, that nothing can be said here which would not be useless repetition.

(5)Second. As to the tenure by which the judges are to hold their places; this chiefly concerns their duration in office; the provisions for their support; the precautions for their responsibility.

(6)According to the plan of the convention, all judges who may be appointed by the United States are to hold their offices DURING w; which is conformable to the most approved of the State method of appointing judges. Second. The conditions of their terms of office. Third. The subdivision of the judicial branch into different courts and the relationship of those courts to each other.

(4)First. The method of appointing judges is the same as the method of appointing any other non-elected official of the federal government.* This has been thoroughly discussed in *The Federalist No. 76* and *77.* Nothing more can be said here that would not be useless repetition.

(5)Second. The conditions of their employment primarily concern the length of their terms of office, who will pay them and how much, and methods for holding them accountable.

(6)According to the new Constitution, all federal judges will hold office for an unlimited amount of time unless they commit some offense

ORIGINAL of FEDERALIST # 78

constitutions and among the rest, to that of this State. Its propriety having been drawn into question by the adversaries of that plan,

is no light symptom of the rage for objection, which disorders their imaginations and judgments.

(7)The standard of good behavior for the continuance in office of the judicial magistracy, is certainly one of the most valuable of the modern improvements in the practice of government. In a monarchy it is an excellent barrier to the despotism of the prince; in a republic it is a no less excellent barrier to the encroachments and oppressions of the representative body. And it is the best expedient which can be devised in any government, to secure a steady, upright, and impartial administration of the laws.

for which they can be impeached. The State constitutions that are most approved of grant the same term of office for their State judges. New York is one of those states. The fact that the opponents of the new government have questioned the wisdom of this, shows that their love of quarreling has warped their imaginations and their judgments.

[7]An unlimited term during good behavior for judges is one of the most valuable modern improvements in the design of government. In a monarchy, it protects judges from the over-reaching power of the king. In a republic, it is no less effective in protecting the judicial branch from being over-powered by the legislative branch. And it is the best solution that can be devised in any government to insure the consistent, honest and impartial management of the laws.

ORIGINAL of FEDERALIST # 78

(8)*Whoever attentively considers the different departments of power must perceive, that, in a government in which they are separated from each other, the judiciary, from the nature of its functions, will always be the least dangerous to the political*

rights of the Constitution; because it will be least in a capacity to annoy or injure them. The Executive not only dispenses the honors, but holds the sword of the community. The legislature not only commands the purse, but prescribes the rules by which the duties and rights of every citizen are to be regulated.

(9)*The judiciary, on the contrary, has no influence over either the sword or the purse; no direction either of the strength or of the wealth of the society; and can take no active resolution whatever. It may truly be said to have neither FORCE nor WILL, but merely judgment; and must ultimately depend upon the aid of the executive arm even for the efficacy of its judgments.*

MODERN version of FEDERALIST # 78

[8]Careful consideration of the different branches of government will reveal that the judicial branch will always be the least dangerous to Constitutional rights because it has the least power with which to threaten them. The executive branch not only appoints officials but also holds the sword of the nation. That is, the President commands the armed forces. The legislature commands the purse. In other words, the Congress controls the financial resources of the nation. Furthermore, Congress writes the laws that determine how the duties and rights of every citizen will be regulated.

[9]The judiciary, on the contrary, has no influence over either the sword or the purse. It controls neither the strength nor the wealth of the nation, and has absolutely no ability to put its decisions into action. It may be truly said that the judiciary has neither force nor will but merely judgment. It must ultimately depend on the

ORIGINAL of FEDERALIST # 78

(10)*This simple view of the matter suggests several important consequences. It proves incontestably, that the judiciary is beyond comparison the weakest of the three departments of power;* that it can never attack with success either of the other two; and that all possible care is requisite to enable it to defend itself against their attacks. It equally proves, that though individual oppression may now and then proceed from the courts of justice, the general liberty of the people can never be endangered from that quarter; I mean so long as the judiciary remains truly distinct from both the legislature and the Executive. For I agree, that "there is no liberty, if the power of judging be not separated from the legislative and executive powers." (Montesquieu, pg 181)*

---

*The celebrated Montesquieu, speaking of them, says "of the three powers above mentioned, the Judiciary is next to nothing." --*Spirit of Laws*, Vol. I, page 186

MODERN version of FEDERALIST # 78

executive branch to insure that its decisions take effect.

[10]A simple view of the matter implies several important consequences. It has been proven that the judiciary is unarguably the weakest of the three branches of government.* It can never successfully attack either of the other two branches. Furthermore a government must be so constructed so that the judicial branch can defend itself from the attacks of the other two. It is equally clear that although an occasional action by a federal court will tend to diminish rights or freedoms of the people, in general their liberty can never be endangered by that branch as long as its powers are truly separated from those of the legislative and executive. I agree that "there is no liberty if the power of judging is not separated from the legislative and executive

ORIGINAL of FEDERALIST # 78

[11]*And it proves, in the last place, that as liberty can have nothing to fear from the judiciary alone, but would have every thing to fear from its union with either of the other departments; that as all the effects of a such a union must ensue from a dependence of the former on the latter, notwithstanding a nominal and apparent separation; that as, from the natural feebleness of the judiciary, it is in continual jeopardy of being overpowered, awed, or influenced by its co-ordinate branches; and that as nothing can contribute so much to its firmness and independence as permanency in office, this quality may therefore be justly regarded as an indispensable ingredient in its constitution, and, in a great measure, as the citadel of the public justice and the public security.*

powers.*   Finally, there are several points to be made in support of permanent terms of office, which would give independence to the judicial branch.

[11]Liberty can have nothing to fear from the judiciary alone and everything to fear from its combination with either of the other branches. The harmful effects of such a combination would result from the dependence of the judicial branch on the other branch.   This harm will result unless the separation between the branches is real and not just apparent.   Because of its weakness, the judicial branch is in constant danger of being overpowered, overawed or overly influenced by the other branches.   Nothing would contribute so much to the stability and independence of the judiciary as permanent terms of office.   In fact, it is correct to

---

*The celebrated Montesquieu, speaking of them, says "of the three powers above mentioned, the Judiciary is next to nothing." --*Spirit of Laws*, Vol. I, page 186

(12)*The complete independence of the courts of justice is peculiarly essential in a limited Constitution. By a limited Constitution, I understand one which contains certain specified exceptions to the legislative authority; such, for instance, as that it shall pass no bills of attainder, no ex-post-facto laws, and the like. Limitations of this kind can be preserved in practice no other way than through the medium of courts of justice, whose duty it must be to declare all acts contrary to the manifest tenor of the Constitution void. Without this, all the reservations of particular rights or privileges would amount to nothing.*

(13)*Some perplexity respecting the rights of the courts to pronounce legislative acts void, because contrary to the Constitution, has arisen from an imagination that the*

MODERN version of FEDERALIST # 78

assume that life terms are the most important component in the structure of the judicial branch. It is primarily this feature that guarantees the protection of justice and order in a society.

[12]The complete independence of the courts of justice is especially important with a Constitution that limits the powers of the legislature. The legislature may not, for example pass bills of attainder, or *ex post facto* laws. However, these limitations will be preserved only by the courts, whose duty it must be to declare all acts invalid that contradict the clear meaning of the Constitution. If the courts do not have this power, all rights guaranteed on paper would amount to nothing.

[13]Some are worried about the courts' ability to find legislative acts unconstitutional because they believe this power implies that the power of the courts is superior to the legislative power. They

ORIGINAL of FEDERALIST # 78

doctrine would imply a superiority of the judiciary to the legislative power. It is urged that the authority which can declare the acts of another void, must necessarily be superior to the one whose acts may be declared void. As this doctrine is of great importance in all the American constitutions, a brief discussion of the ground on which it rests cannot be unacceptable.

(14)There is no position which depends on clearer principles, than that every act of a delegated authority, contrary to the tenor of the commission under which it is exercised, is void. No legislative act, therefore, contrary to the Constitution, can be valid. To deny this, would be to affirm, that the deputy is greater than his principal; that the servant is above his master; that the representatives of the people are superior to the people themselves; that men acting by virtue of powers, may do not only what their powers do not authorize, but what they forbid.

MODERN version of FEDERALIST # 78

insist that when one part of government can overturn the acts of another part of the government, it must necessarily possess a superior authority. As the power of judicial review (the power to declare laws unconstitutional) is of great importance both in the States' constitutions as well as in the new federal Constitution, a brief justification of it is appropriate.

[14]When the action of a person, or group, to whom power has been given, contradicts the meaning of the document that gave them that power, then that action is invalid. There is no position that is more clearly justified. No law, therefore, which contradicts the Constitution, can be valid. To deny this would be to claim that the deputy is greater than his superior; that the servant is above the master; that the representatives of the people are superior to the people themselves; that men who have been given certain powers may not

ORIGINAL of FEDERALIST # 78

(15)*If it be said that the legislative body are themselves the constitutional judges of their own powers, and that the construction they put upon them is conclusive upon the other departments, it may be answered, that this cannot be the natural*

not otherwise to be supposed, that the Constitution could intend to enable the representatives of the people to substitute their WILL to that of their constituents.

(16)*It is far more rational to suppose, that the courts were designed to be an intermediate body between the people and the legislature, in order, among other things, to keep the latter within the limits assigned to their authority. The interpretation of the laws is the proper and peculiar province of the courts. A constitution is, in fact, and must be regarded by the*

only take unauthorized actions but may actually do what those powers forbid.

[15]Some would claim that the members of the legislature are themselves the correct judges of their own powers according to the Constitution. Furthermore, their interpretation of the Constitution is final and the other two branches are obliged to follow it. However this cannot be automatically assumed since it is not found in any part of the text of the Constitution. There is no reason to suppose that the Constitution intends that the will of the elected representatives be substituted for the will of the people.

[16]It is far more rational to suppose that the courts were designed to mediate between the people and the legislature to insure, among other things, that the legislature stay within the Constitutional limits of its authority. The interpretation of the laws

ORIGINAL of FEDERALIST # 78

judges, as a fundamental law. It therefore belongs to them to ascertain its meaning, as well as the meaning of any particular act proceeding from the legislative body. If there should happen to be an irreconcilable variance between the two, that which has the superior obligation and validity ought, of course, to be preferred; or, in other words, the Constitution ought to be preferred to the statute, the intention of the people to the intention of their agents.

(17)Nor does this conclusion by any means suppose a superiority of the judicial to the legislative power. It only supposes that the power of the people is superior to both; and that where the will of the legislature, declared in its statutes, stands in opposition to that of the people, declared in the Constitution, the judges ought to be governed by the latter rather than the former. They

is the proper and special function of the courts. A constitution is the fundamental law, the basis of all other laws, and must be treated as such by the judges. It is therefore their responsibility to determine its meaning as well as the meaning of any law passed by the legislature. If there is a direct contradiction between a law and the Constitution, the one which is more valid and to which we owe the most loyalty ought to be chosen. In other words, the Constitution must be given preference over the statute, the will of the people must prevail over the will of their representatives.

[17]This does not imply that the judiciary is superior to the legislative power, but that the power of the people is superior to both. So that, if the will of the legislature expressed in its law opposes the will of the people declared in the Constitution, the judges ought to abide by the will of the people. Their

ORIGINAL of FEDERALIST # 78

ought to regulate their decisions by the fundamental laws, rather than by those which are not fundamental.

[18]This exercise of judicial discretion, in determining between two contradictory laws, is exemplified in a familiar instance. It not uncommonly happens, that there are two statutes existing at one time, clashing in whole or in part with each other, and neither of them containing any repealing clause or expression. In such a case, it is the province of the courts to liquidate and fix their meaning and operation. So far as they can, by any fair construction, be reconciled to each other, reason and law conspire to dictate that this should be done; where this is impracticable, it becomes a matter of necessity to give effect to one, in exclusion of the other. The rule which has obtained in the courts for determining their relative validity is, that the last in order of time shall be preferred to the first. But this is a mere rule of construction, not derived from any positive

decisions ought to be guided only by laws that form a foundation for all other laws.

[18]The ability of courts to decide between two laws can be illustrated by the following example. It sometimes happens that there are two laws that wholly or partially contradict each other and neither law contains a provision indicating how such a contradiction should be solved. It is the responsibility of the court to solve the problem by determining the meaning of the law and its application. If it is possible through any honest interpretation of the two laws, each should be preserved. Both reason and law demand this. But where this is impractical, it becomes necessary to uphold one law and abolish the other. The rule that courts have used in the past is that the most recently passed law should be upheld and the older law rejected. But this is merely the sensible solution to a practical problem, not a rule derived from a

ORIGINAL of FEDERALIST # 78

law, but from the nature and reason of the thing. It is a rule not enjoined upon the courts by legislative provision, but adopted by themselves, as consonant to truth and propriety, for the direction of their conduct as interpreters of the law. They thought it reasonable, that between the interfering acts of an EQUAL authority, that which was the last indication of its will should have the preference.

[19]But in regard to the interfering acts of a superior and subordinate authority, of an original and derivative power, the nature and reason of the thing indicate the converse of that rule as proper to be followed. They teach us that the prior act of a superior ought to be preferred to the subsequent act of an inferior and subordinate authority; and that accordingly, whenever a particular statute contravenes the Constitution, it will be the duty of the judicial tribunals to adhere to the latter and disregard the former.

written law. It is not a rule imposed on the courts by the legislature. Instead, because this rule is realistic and appropriate, courts have adopted it for themselves. They thought it was reasonable that when two laws issued by the same legislature contradicted each other, the most recent law most accurately reflected what the lawmakers intended and so should be given preference over the older law.

[19]But when different legislatures -- one higher having primary authority and the other having power derived from that higher authority -- issue two contradictory laws, the opposite rule should apply. It is reasonable and appropriate in this situation that the older law passed by the higher legislature should be followed rather than the more recent act of the lower legislature. It is equally correct that whenever a particular law conflicts with

ORIGINAL of FEDERALIST # 78

[20]*It can be of no weight to say that the courts, on the pretense of a repugnancy, may substitute their own pleasure to the constitutional intentions of the legislature. This might as well happen in the case of two contradictory statutes; or it might as well happen in every adjudication upon any single statute. The courts must declare the sense of the law; and if they should be disposed to exercise WILL instead of JUDGMENT, the consequence would equally be the substitution of their pleasure to that of the legislative body. The observation, if it prove any thing, would prove that there ought to be no judges distinct from that body.*

[21]*If, then, the courts of justice are to be considered as the bulwarks of a limited Constitution against legislative encroachments, this consideration will afford a strong argument for the permanent tenure of judicial*

the Constitution, it is the duty of the judiciary to uphold the Constitution and to disregard that law.

[20]It is pointless to claim that the courts may use their power to find a law unconstitutional in order to substitute their own desires for the rightful intentions of the legislature. That could just as well occur when laws passed by two different legislatures contradict each other, or when the courts are merely interpreting a single law. The courts must interpret the meaning of the law. If they ever wish to impose their will rather than using their judgment, the result will always be the substitution of whatever they may want for the desires of the legislature. If this argument proves anything at all, it proves that there should never be any judge independent from the legislature.

[21]However, if the courts are to be considered a fortification against the expansion of legislative power, then there is a strong argument for the

ORIGINAL of FEDERALIST # 78

offices, since nothing will contribute so much as this to that independent spirit in the judges which must be essential to the faithful performance of so arduous a duty.

(22)This independence of the judges is equally requisite to guard the Constitution and the rights of individuals from the effects of those ill humors, which the arts of designing men, or the influence of particular conjunctures, sometimes disseminate among the people themselves, and which, though they speedily give place to better information, and more deliberate reflection, have a tendency, in the meantime, to occasion dangerous innovations in the government, and serious oppressions of the minor party in the community.

(23)Though I trust the friends of the proposed Constitution will never concur with its enemies, in questioning that fundamental principle of republican

THE FEDERALIST PAPERS: A Modern Translation in Parallel Text

MODERN version of FEDERALIST # 78

permanent term of office for judges. Nothing else will contribute so much to that independent spirit in judges which is essential to the reliable performance of such difficult duties.

[22]The independence of judges is equally important in guarding the Constitution and individual rights from occasional public anger spread either by the cunning of deceitful men or arising from an unfortunate coincidence of events. Even though this type of public displeasure quickly disappears once the truth is known and people have had time to think more carefully about it, in the meantime it can lead to dangerous changes in the government and the oppression of minorities in the community.

[23]I am sure that the friends of the new Constitution will never agree with its enemies when they question one of the fundamental beliefs of republican government, which asserts the right of

ORIGINAL of FEDERALIST # 78

government, which admits the right of the people to alter or abolish the established Constitution, whenever they find it inconsistent with their happiness, yet it is not to be inferred from this principle, that the representatives of the people, whenever a momentary inclination happens to lay hold of a majority of their constituents, incompatible with the provisions in the existing Constitution, would, on that account, be justifiable in a violation of those provisions; or that the courts would be under a greater obligation to connive at infractions in this shape, than when they had proceeded wholly from the cabals of the representative body.

(24)Until the people have, by some solemn and authoritative act, annulled or changed the established form, it is binding upon themselves collectively, as well as individually; and no presumption, or even knowledge, of their sentiments, can warrant their representatives in a their departure from it, prior to such an act. But it is

the people to alter or abolish an existing constitution whenever they find that it does not promote their well-being. Yet this principle should not be interpreted to mean that the representatives of the people are justified in violating the existing constitution whenever a majority of the people they represent are possessed by a temporary bias. Nor does it mean that the courts should overlook violations by legislators who are following the mood of the public any more than they should overlook violations that arise entirely from plots by legislators.

[24]Until the people have, by some solemn and official action, cancelled or changed the established constitution, they are bound individually and collectively to uphold it. No assumption of, or even knowledge of, the people's desires can justify unconstitutional actions by their representatives

ORIGINAL of FEDERALIST # 78

easy sentiments, can warrant their representatives in a departure from it, prior to such an act. But it is easy to see that it would require an uncommon portion of fortitude in the judges to do their duty as faithful guardians of the Constitution, where legislative invasions of it had been instigated by the major voice of the community.

(25)But it is not with a view to infractions of the Constitution only, that the independence of the judges may be an essential safeguard against the effects of occasional ill humors in the society. These sometimes extend no farther than to the injury of the private rights of particular classes of citizens, by unjust and partial laws. Here also the firmness of the judicial magistracy is of vast importance in mitigating the severity and confining the operation of such laws. It not only serves

MODERN version of FEDERALIST # 78

canceling or altering their constitution. But it is easy to see that it would require uncommon courage on the part of judges to do their duty as faithful guardians of the Constitution when violations of it by legislators had been made in response to the expressed wishes of a majority of the people.

[25]But it is not only in regard to violations of the Constitution that an independent judiciary will act as a safeguard against occasional public anger. Violations of the Constitution sometimes injure only the private rights of particular groups of citizens by unjust or unequal laws. A strong judiciary is essential in reducing the harm caused by such laws and in limiting their use. A strong judiciary not only serves to moderate the harm caused by laws, which may have already been passed, but it also acts as a restraint on the

ORIGINAL of FEDERALIST # 78

to moderate the immediate mischiefs of those which may have been passed, but it operates as a check upon the legislative body in passing them; who, perceiving that obstacles to the success of iniquitous intention are to be expected from the scruples of the courts, are in a manner compelled, by the very motives of the injustice they meditate, to qualify their attempts.

(26)This is a circumstance calculated to have more influence upon the character of our governments, than but few may be aware of. The benefits of the integrity and moderation of the judiciary have already been felt in more States than one; and though they may have displeased those whose sinister expectations they may have disappointed, they must have commanded the esteem and applause of all the virtuous and disinterested. Considerate men, of every description, ought to prize whatever will tend to beget or fortify that temper in the legislature to prevent them from passing such laws in the first place. They will no longer desire to achieve their unjust cause when they see that the success of their dishonorable intentions will be blocked by a conscientious judiciary.

[26]This feature of the new Constitution is calculated to have more of an influence on the essential quality of the government than most people realize. More than one State has already experienced the benefits of having an honest and moderating judiciary. And, although the judiciary may have displeased those whose sinister plans they thwarted, they must also have received the respect and appreciation of all who are virtuous and fair. Reasonable men of all descriptions ought to prize whatever will strengthen the qualities of moderation

ORIGINAL of FEDERALIST # 78

courts: as no man can be sure that he may not be to-morrow the victim of a spirit of injustice, by which he may be a gainer to-day. And every man must now feel, that the inevitable tendency of such a spirit is to sap the foundations of public and private confidence, and to introduce in its stead universal distrust and distress.

[27]That inflexible and uniform adherence to the rights of the Constitution, and of individuals, which we perceive to be indispensable in the courts of justice, can certainly not be expected from judges who hold their offices by a temporary commission. Periodical appointments, however regulated, or by whomsoever made, would, in some way or other, be fatal to their necessary independence. If the power of making them was committed either to the Executive or legislature, there would be danger of an improper complaisance to the branch which possessed it; if to both, there would be an unwillingness to hazard the displeasure of either;

and integrity in the courts. No one can be sure that he will not be the victim of the same injustice tomorrow by which he was the winner today. And everyone must now feel that the inevitable result of this insecurity is to weaken the foundations of national and individual confidence and to replace it with a general sense of distrust and distress.

[27]The inflexible and unchanging devotion to Constitutional rights and to natural rights, which we consider indispensable in the courts of justice, certainly cannot be expected from judges who hold their offices by temporary appointment. Appointment to a limited term, regardless of how or by whom it is made, would in some way or another be fatal to the independence of the judiciary. If either the executive or the legislative branch held the power to make limited judicial appointments, there is a danger that the court would tend to yield improperly to that branch. If

ORIGINAL of FEDERALIST # 78

if to the people, or to persons chosen by them for the special purpose, there would be too great a disposition to consult popularity, to justify a reliance that nothing would be consulted but the Constitution and the laws.

(28)There is yet a further and a weightier reason for the permanency of the judicial offices, which is deducible from the nature of the qualifications they require. It has been frequently remarked, with great propriety, that a voluminous code of laws is one of the inconveniences necessarily connected with the advantages of a free government. To avoid an arbitrary discretion in the courts, it is indispensable that they should be bound down by strict rules and precedents, which serve to define and point out their duty in every particular case that comes before them; and it will readily be conceived from the variety of controversies which grow out of the folly

that power were given to the people or to representatives chosen by the people for this special purpose, there would be too great a tendency to consult popular opinion when making a decision that should only be made by consulting the Constitution and the law.

[28]There is another important reason for the permanency of judicial officers that can be determined from the qualifications these jobs require. It has been often and truly said that having a great quantity of laws is one of the disadvantages that accompany the advantages of a free government. It is essential that judges be restrained by strict rules and precedents, which clarify and define their duty in every individual case that comes before them, so that they will not make arbitrary decisions. It is easy to understand from the variety of court cases that result from the foolishness and

ORIGINAL of FEDERALIST # 78

and wickedness of mankind, that the records of those precedents must unavoidably swell to a very considerable bulk, and must demand long and laborious study to acquire a competent knowledge of them. Hence it is, that there can be but few men in the society who will have sufficient skill in the laws to qualify them for the stations of judges. And making the proper deductions for the ordinary depravity of human nature, the number must be still smaller of those who unite the requisite integrity with the requisite knowledge.

(29)These considerations apprise us, that the government can have no great option between fit character; and that a temporary duration in office, which would naturally discourage such characters from quitting a lucrative line of practice to accept a seat on the bench, would have a tendency to throw the administration of justice into hands less able, and less well qualified, to

wickedness of mankind that the records of these previous cases must inevitably increase to a considerable number. It is clear that acquiring a competent knowledge of all of these cases would require long and difficult study. Hence, there will be only a few men in any society who will have sufficient skills to qualify them for the position of a judge. Taking into account the weaknesses of human nature, the number of people who will have both the necessary skills and the necessary integrity is even smaller.

[29]Considering these facts we see that there will be few suitable men of good character for the government to choose from. A short term of office would discourage many qualified men from leaving well-paid law practices to accept a judgeship. This would tend to place the administration of justice into hands less capable and less qualified to carry it

conduct it utility and dignity. In the present circumstances of this country, and in those in which it is likely to be for a long time to come, the disadvantages on this score would be greater than they may at first sight appear; but it must be confessed, that they are far inferior to those which present themselves under the other aspects of the subject.

(30)Upon the whole, there can be no room to doubt that the convention acted wisely in copying from the models of those constitutions which have established GOOD BEHAVIOR *as the tenure of their judicial offices, in point of duration; and that so far from being blamable on this account, their plan would have been inexcusably defective, if it had wanted this important feature of good government. The experience of Great Britain affords an illustrious comment on the excellence of the institution.*   PUBLIUS

out with dignity and for the benefit of the public. In the present condition of this country, and the condition it is likely to be in for a long time to come, the problem of not attracting the most qualified men is more serious than you might think. However, it must be admitted that the other disadvantages caused by limited terms of office are even more serious.

[30]When all aspects of this subject are considered, there can be no doubt that the Philadelphia convention acted wisely in using as models those constitutions that establish unlimited terms for their judicial offices. Instead of being blamed for this, their plan would have been inexcusably flawed if it had excluded this important feature of good government. The experience of Great Britain provides a shining example of the excellence of unlimited terms.

Friend of PUBLIUS

RESEARCH AND DISCUSSION QUESTIONS for *Federalist # 78*

1. The authors of the Constitution and of the Federalist Papers were concerned that federal judges and Justices of the Supreme Court be impartial and beyond the reach of politics. They believed that the Constitution ensured that independence. Does the recent history of the Supreme Court suggest that Justices of the Supreme Court are not influenced by political or ideological points of view?

2. The Framers were also concerned that the judicial branch of the national government should be independent of public opinion. Does recent history show that they are or are not influenced by public opinion?

3. Some legal scholars suggest that setting term limits for Justices of the Supreme Court that expire at definite intervals will prevent too many Justices from being appointed by the same President, also ensuring that the Court isn't too far out of step with current conditions in the country. What would Hamilton think of this suggestion given what he has written about term limits in general? (Federalist # 70)

4. The Constitution does not specify qualifications for Justices such as age, education, profession, or native-born citizenship. A Justice does not have to be a lawyer or a law school graduate. Should requirements be added

to ensure that only the most qualified individuals are appointed to the Court?

5. Election of judges has been instituted in some States. What are the pros and cons of elected as opposed to appointed judges.

The Constitution is a relatively brief outline compared to the complex governmental structure it creates. Its provisions have required many judicial interpretations since it was formally approved in 1788.

GLOSSARY

****

accountability. *noun.* The condition of being answerable or responsible. If we say, for example, that "there is more accountability with a single official than with a group of officials," we mean that when there is only one person, we know who to blame if something goes wrong.

annual. *adjective.* Yearly or once a year. Annual elections are elections that are held once a year.

Articles of Confederation. The first constitution of the United States. It was ratified in 1781. *The Articles of Confederation* are sometimes referred to as "the *Articles.*" That document established a weak central government for the newly independent thirteen States. It was replaced when our present constitution was ratified in 1789.

check. *verb.* To stop or slow down. To restrain. In the system of government established by the Constitution, each branch has the power to stop or restrain the other branches.

Commerce. noun. The buying and selling of goods especially on a large scale. This word is often used to describe all the business activities of a nation or state. For example, the "Commerce Clause" is a part of the Constitution that gives Congress the power to regulate all the business that is conducted across state lines or across the nation's borders.

confederacy. *noun.* Also sometimes called a "confederation." An alliance or league. A government created when independent nation-states create a central government with few and limited powers. The United States under the *Articles of Confederation* was a confederacy or confederation. The southern states that broke off from the rest of the U.S. in 1861 formed a confederation. The United Nations is a modern example of a confederacy or confederation.

confederate. *adjective.* United in a confederacy. Sometimes used as a verb **to confederate**, meaning to join in a confederation.

constitution. *noun.* The basic, fundamental law of a nation. It usually describes the plan of government, how the government is to be divided, which parts of the government are to have which powers, etc. Constitutions also sometimes list and describe the basic rights of citizens. Not all constitutions exist as single documents. The constitution of the UK is made up of several documents and some long-standing traditions.

co-presidents. *noun.* The prefix "co" means jointly or together. Co-presidents are two or more people who govern together as the chief executive officers.

demagogue. *noun.* A person who gains political power by appealing to the emotions. Prejudices and fears of average people. Adolf Hitler was a demagogue. Some historians say that so was Joseph McCarthy.

democracy. *noun.* In the words of Abraham Lincoln, "a government of the people, by the people, for the people." A government in which the will of the people determines the decisions of government either directly through their votes or indirectly by the votes of their representatives.

divisiveness. *noun.* The quality of being divisive, of creating divisions or dissent. Something that creates divisiveness turns groups of people against each other. It the opposite of creating unity or harmony.

elite. *noun.* A superior or privileged group Usually the same as the upper-class in a society although it sometimes just means those who have superior intelligence or talent. In political science, "the elite" often means those who use their wealth to gain and hold on to political power. This is the meaning of the phrase as it is used in *Federalist #39*.

executive. *noun.* The person, or part of government, who has the duty to carry out the laws. To put the laws into effect. The legislative branch writes the law but it is up to the executive branch to turn the words of the law into action.

faction. *noun.* A group of people united by an interest that is at odds with the common interest. Similar to the way a fraction is part of a whole, a faction is part of a whole group. The term faction usually has a negative connotation. As the smaller group pursues goals related to their interest, conflict often occurs with the larger group.

factious. *adjective.* Something is factious if it divides groups of people against each other creating disunity and disharmony.

federal. *adjective.* A form of government in which authority to govern is shared, more or less equally, between a central government and member states. To Madison, Hamilton, and Jay, federal and confederate meant the same thing. After the *Constitution of 1787* was adopted, federal came to mean the kind of government that it created. Confederate now means the kind of government that the U.S. had under the Articles of Confederation. Compare federal to the definition of confederate above.

fundamental. *adjective.* Basic and most mportant. For example, the Constitution is the fundamental law of our nation. That is to say, the Constitution is the most important law and it provides a foundation for all other laws.

impeachment. *noun.* An official accusation of wrongdoing by the House of Representatives directed at the President or a federal judge. The House can pass an Article of Impeachment, detailing the wrongdoing, by a majority vote. A trial is then held in the Senate. The Chief Justice of the Supreme Court is the presiding judge in this trial. If two-thirds of the Senate vote guilty on an Article of Impeachment, the President (or judge) is removed from office.

international law. The law that governs the conduct between nations or between a nation and a foreign citizen or between citizens of different countries. It is really a combination of three things: (1) treaties between countries, (2) customs and (3) generally accepted principles of law. An example of a treaty would be the Treaty of Paris that ended the Revolutionary War. An example of custom would be the custom of allowing governments to negotiate peace treaties on behalf of their citizens. An accepted principle of law would be that piracy is theft and it is wrong even when it occurs on the high seas (that is, outside of the territorial jurisdiction of any nation).

judicial. *adjective.* Of or pertaining to the judiciary branch, courts of law or the justice system in general.

judicial review. The power of courts to find laws unconstitutional. The power of judicial review allows a court to declare a law or any governmental action invalid because it conflicts with the fundamental law of the Constitution. Today, any court that keeps a verbatim (exact word for word) record of each case it hears has the power of judicial review. However, the U.S. Supreme Court has final judicial review of laws that may conflict with the U.S. Constitution.

judiciary branch. One of the three major divisions of government. The judiciary branch runs the court system, interprets the law, and hears cases when disputes arise or when the executive branch believes a law has been broken.

legislate. *verb.* To make laws. To write, revise and vote on proposed laws.

legislation. *noun* Another term for a "bill" before it is finalized, or a "law" after it is finalized.

legislative. *adjective.* Of or pertaining to a legislature or law-making body.

legislator. *noun.* A person who legislates (makes laws).

legislature. *noun.* An officially elected or appointed group of people who are responsible for making laws.

liberty. *noun.* Freedom. The state of being able to act according to one's own wishes.

majority. *noun.* More than half of the total number. A majority is a group made up of more than half of the members of the whole group. A simple majority is any number that is more than fifty-one percent (51%). A super-majority is two-thirds or three-fourths of the whole number.

minority. *noun.* Less than half the whole number. A group made up of less than half of the whole group. Latino-, African-, and Asian Americans are considered members of ethnic minority groups because none of these groups is larger than half of the whole population of the U.S. Groups of people who share the same opinion can be considered a minority if they constitute less than fifty percent of the whole. Madison and Hamilton used the word minority to mean a small group that shared a common opinion or interest.

moderate. *adjective.* Opposed to radical or extreme views. For example, someone who is ideologically moderate is neither very conservative nor very liberal.

Parliament. *proper noun.* The legislature of the United Kingdom. It is made up of two houses, the House of Lords and the House of Commons. Parliament with a small "p" (parliament) refers to any legislature in which the chief executive (the Prime Minister) sits as a member. This is different from our system of separated powers wherein the chief executive (the President) is not allowed to also be a member of the legislature.

Philadelphia Convention. A meeting of appointed delegates from the states, it was organized for the sole purpose of revising the Articles of Confederation. Within two weeks of convening in May 1787, the Virginia delegation proposed a wholly new constitution. Thus the meeting became known as the "Constitutional Convention."

popular government. noun. Government of the people. A democracy. The "popular" comes from the Latin word popularis, which means "of the people."

precedents. plural noun. In general use "precedent" means something that came before. In legal usage, a precedent is a law or case that serves as a model to use in judging all similar cases in the future.

private sector. noun. That part of society that is not owned or administered by the government. The opposite term is "public sector," that part of a nation's economy that is owned and/or run by the government.

proverb. *noun.* A short saying that expresses a well-accepted opinion.

the public good. The public good is that which best serves the interests of the people. This is the way that Madison and Hamilton use the term. Please notice that there is a difference between **the public good** and **a public good**. A public good is something like clean air or street lighting that everyone benefits from and which it is difficult to charge people for according to how much they benefit. A public good is usually therefore paid for by a general tax.

pure democracy. A government in which the will of the people is expressed directly by them. Every important law is voted on directly by the public. Compare the meaning of **pure democracy** to the meaning of **republic** below.

ratification. *noun.* The act of officially approving of a treaty or a constitution. The Constitution of 1787 (our current constitution) was ratified by a vote of delegates to special ratifying conventions called in every state. Three-fourths of the states' ratifying conventions had to ratify (officially approve) the Constitution before it became law.

republic. *noun.* A government in which the people select representatives to make laws and execute the laws for them. Compare the meaning of **republic** to the meaning of **pure democracy** above.

republican government. The government of a republic. See **republic** above.

sects. *noun.* A distinct group of people, within a larger group, who are different from the larger group because of their beliefs or practices. This term is usually used when describing religious groups.

sovereignty. *noun.* Possession of the highest governing authority within a territory. Supreme authority to govern. In a federal system sovereignty is shared between the national government (what we call the federal government) and the states' governments.

sphere of power. The area in which a government has jurisdiction. This may or may not be a geographical area. For example, some have described the federal system as two overlapping spheres of power. The federal government and the State governments have responsibility for the same people and the same territory, but each has its own sphere of power. The federal government has the power to declare war and peace in order to protect the nation. The State governments have the power to create school systems within the same territory in order to provide for the welfare of the people.

State assembly. The lower house of the legislature of most State governments is called an assembly.

term of office. The length of time an official is elected or appointed to serve. When his/her term of office is over he/she may be re-elected or re-appointed. For example, the term of office for a U.S. Representative is two years. The term of office of a U.S. Senator is six years.

tyranny. *noun.* A government in which a ruler has absolute power which he uses in a cruel, harsh or arbitrary manner. No law constrains him and no civil rights are protected.

tyrant. *noun.* A person who rules with unlimited powers that he/she uses in a cruel, harsh or arbitrary manner. The American colonists accused George III of being a tyrant because he suspended their legislatures, closed ports and taxed them without their consent Today we would probably use the term "dictator" rather than tyrant.

unitary government. A government in which all important powers belong to the central (national) government. Local governments exist but have a limited ability to make laws or decisions for themselves. They are answerable to the central government. Most of the world's governments are unitary. The governments of the U.K. and Japan are examples of unitary governments.

unity. *noun.* The condition of being one, or being a single thing. Madison says that unity in the presidency makes decision-making more efficient. The fact that the President is a single person means that he can make decisions faster than if the presidency was split between two or more people.

unlimited government. A government whose powers are not defined by law and whose actions are not constrained by law. An absolute monarchy or a dictatorship would both be examples of unlimited government.

Made in the USA
Las Vegas, NV
20 December 2023

83190120R00181